£ 30

Poems of Olga Orozco, Marosa di Giorgio & Jorge Palma

Acknowledgements

Several of these translations have appeared in the following journals:
Cordite, Mascara, Shearsman (UK), *Southerly*.

The original poems of Olga Orozco were published in Olga Orozco,
Poesía completa, Adriana Hidalgo editora, Buenos Aires, 2012. The poems
by Marosa di Giorgio were published in *Los papeles salvajes*, Adriana
Hidalgo editores, Buenos Aires, 2008. Copyright for the original poems
by Jorge Palma lies with the author.

With special thanks to Adriana Hidalgo editora for their assistance in
obtaining permission for publishing the translations of Olga Orozco
and Marosa di Giorgio. With special thanks also to Nidia di Giorgio
and Jorge Palma for their support in this project.

Poems of Olga Orozco, Marosa di Giorgio & Jorge Palma
The Americas Poetry Series 1

First published 2017 by Vagabond Press
PO Box 958 Newtown NSW 2042 Australia
www.vagabondpress.net

Olga Orozco, Marosa di Giorgio & Jorge Palma © 2016
English translations, Peter Boyle © 2017

Cover image © Stuart Cooke, 2015. (Holiday Cottage, Cabo Polonio, Uruguay)
Designed and typeset by Michael Brennan.

ISBN 978-1-922181-80-0

Poems of Olga Orozco, Marosa di Giorgio & Jorge Palma

Translated from Spanish and introduced by Peter Boyle

Vagabond Press | The Americas Poetry Series

CONTENTS

Introduction by Peter Boyle ... 7

OLGA OROZCO

Cartomancy ... 25

Genesis ... 31

For Emilio in his Heaven ... 35

Cantos to Berenice (V) ... 37

Cantos to Berenice (VI) ... 39

Cantos to Berenice (VII) ... 40

Cantos to Berenice (IX) ... 41

Cantos to Berenice (XIV) ... 42

Cantos to Berenice (XVII) ... 44

Masks doubling everything ... 45

Between dog and wolf ... 47

Pavane for a dead princess ... 49

Mutations of Reality ... 52

The Submerged Continent ... 56

Interrogation of a bird through its song ... 58

Animal that breathes ... 60

In the depths, the sun ... 62

It comes back when the rain ... 65

MAROSA DI GIORGIO

from *The Moth* (1987)

Funeral carriages laden with watermelons ... 69

The moth ... 89

JORGE PALMA

Paraphernalia ... 119

The birth of the moon ... 121

The drowned ... 123

The working class don't go to paradise ... 126

Immortals ... 128

Salaries ... 132

Child and leopard ... 133

Florence ... 136

The lighthouse at the end of the world ... 139

Everyday life ... 140

Wide river with autumn fragrance ... 141

Narcissus and the rubbish dump ... 146

Afterwards ... 148

About the authors and translator ... 150

THREE POETS FROM ARGENTINA AND URUGUAY: AN INTRODUCTION

Argentina and Uruguay stand out as countries that have produced an extraordinary range of powerful, original poetry in the 20th Century. To select thirty poets from there would require serious omissions and arbitrary choices. With three poets there can at least be no pretence of representation. I have simply focussed on three poets who appeal strongly to me, all relatively unknown outside Latin America and with either none or only a fraction of their complete work translated into English. As it happens, they come from three distinct generations: Olga Orozco published her first collection of poetry in 1946, Marosa di Giorgio's first collection appeared in 1953 and Jorge Palma's in 1989.

These three poets also exemplify, very loosely, three different approaches to poetry, three important (very loose) lineages within Latin American poetry. With her interest in dreams, prophecy, magic, the poem as inward quest, Argentine poet Olga Orozco (1920-1999) reveals a strong affinity with aspects of Surrealism and German Romanticism. The Argentine Generation of 1940 to which she belonged were powerfully influenced by French Surrealism, but it was not the surrealism of automatic writing or language games that appealed to them. Rather they were drawn to the mysterious, the magical, surrealism's desire to take the poem to unexpected places, its image of the poem as a search for revelation. While Marosa di Giorgio (1932-2007) shares with Orozco a fascination with the oneiric and the magical, her work is more experimental, very much *sui generis*, pushing at the frontier between prose narrative and lyric poetry. Di Giorgio was included in the anthology of neo-baroque poetry *Medusario* (1996), a gathering of highly diverse poets from across Latin America, all marked in different ways by a preference for complexity and disruption, for rich textures and the blurring of genres and language levels. Preceding the neo-baroque movement but also side by side with it, there has been a tradition of more direct, conversational or plain-speaking poetry, associated with Nicaraguan Ernesto Cardenal, the Salvadoran Roque Dalton and the Uruguayan Mario Benedetti, an approach to poetry largely focussed on delivering social-political messages. As with any broad-brush description of poetic movements, this characterization of the neo-baroque and of conversational poetry (also called "the colloquialists") obscures much that is important. Within the neo-baroque grouping there are poets of political witness like Raúl Zurita and there is often a fine sense of humour and a high level of artistry among the more conversational poets. While Jorge Palma (1961-) is interested above all in a socially and politically engaged poetry that speaks directly to the reader, his poems are highly crafted, rich in imagery and rhythmic effects. They invite us, not in any facile way, to think and to feel, to open up to a clearer vision of our world.

Born in 1920 in the small provincial town of Toay, Olga Orozco was the daughter of a Sicilian father and a mother with Basque and Irish ancestry. Her Irish grandmother had, in Orozco's words, "a rather magical, rather animist view of the world" and told stories of spirits, fairies and demons. She prepared magic teas with seven herbs, called in curanderas to treat illnesses and protected and fed wandering mad people like La Lora who believed she was the Virgin Mary and La Reina Genoveva who walked the roads constantly in all weathers. (As a writer Orozco used her mother's maiden name as if to highlight her close affinity with her mother and grandmother.) Toay where she spent her earliest years is a small remote township in the middle of a dry plain of shifting sandhills, immense horizons, flat land far from the sea. At eight she moved with her family to the coastal city of Bahía Blanca, then at sixteen to Buenos Aires. As an adolescent she was immersed in books, chiefly the European classics – Dostoyevski, Dante, Leopardi, and many others.

On leaving school Orozco went to university, married at 19, separated at 24, and all the while was finding her own way into poetry. In these years her poetic influences included Michaux, Rimbaud, Nerval, Quevedo, Cernuda, Rilke, Hörderlin, Oscar V. L. Milosz and others. She collaborated in the production of various student poetry reviews and had several poems published there, but the poetry gathered in her first collection was only begun in 1941. Five years later in 1946 her first collection *Desde lejos* appeared. "For Emilio in his heaven" comes from this collection – it is based on a dream she had of her brother Emilio who died of tuberculosis at age nineteen when she was six. The speed with which Orozco found her own style and the consistency of her poetry across a long life are outstanding. As if to illustrate this, three poems in this selection are from *Los juegos peligrosos* (1962), three from *Museo salvaje* (1974), six from *Cantos a Berenice* (1977), two from *Mutaciones de la realidad* (1979), one from *En el reves del cielo* (1987), and two from her posthumous collection *Ultimos poemas*.

Between 1947 and 1954 Orozco performed in radio dramas as well as translating Italian and French plays. In 1954 she travelled to Brazil, Peru, Ecuador and Chile, meeting various poets and writers. In 1961 she received a scholarship to study "The occult and the sacred in modern poetry", spending nine months travelling in Spain, Italy, France and Switzerland. In Paris she became good friends with fellow Argentines Alejandra Pizarnik and Julio Cortázar, as well as meeting Octavio Paz, Gastón Bachelard and Georges Bataille. A close friendship developed with the younger poet Alejandra Pizarnik who suicided in Buenos Aires in September 1972. "Pavane for a dead princess", dedicated to Alejandra was published in *Mutaciones de la realidad* (1979). In an interview with Jacobo Sefamí, Orozco explains the phrase "Talitha cumi" as the words Jesus spoke to Jairus' daughter, "Little girl, get up" and the phrase "in the depths of everything there is a garden" as a saying her Irish grandmother repeated to her.

Museo salvaje (1974) gathers poems written out of various extreme fears, largely centred around her own body, and a sense of her own unreality. Orozco felt compelled to write poems about parts of her body but, as she did so, problems happened. After writing "My skeleton", for example, she fell and broke two ribs, and after writing a poem dedicated to the eye she developed problems with her sight. "I wanted to be done with the book", she told Sefamí, "so I wouldn't end up having to write it with the remnants of myself, with my last ground-down fragments." "Genesis", "The submerged continent" and "Animal that breathes" come from this collection.

The reality of the magical and supernatural to Orozco is also apparent in the 17 poem sequence *Cantos a Berenice*, dedicated to her cat who had died. Unusually for Orozco, a slow writer, the sequence was completed in an intense two months. Orozco explained in her interview with Sefamí: "Of course she wasn't a cat, she was my totem. She had special powers. I think I wrote much better when Berenice was beside me . . . She died aged fifteen and a half. She had very strange games. She liked to unfold newspapers, to get underneath them and, hidden like that, to walk around everywhere. She kept me warm. In winter, when it was cold, she was like a fox round my neck. I never had another cat. Never wanted one." Orozco was born on March 17 and considered 17 her magic number – *Cantos a Berenice* and two of her other collections contain 17 poems. Bubastis, referred to in poem V, is the town in ancient Egypt where the mummies of cats were buried.

The symbols and emblems of cartomancy, omens, magic and dreams recur across Orozco's poems and it is destiny, fate, fortune or luck that most animates her poetry – the sense of those forces beyond our control that bring us our unique death and whatever love, happiness or suffering we encounter. Magic and omens figure in her poetry not arbitrarily but because, from childhood on, they were so much the very fabric of her life.

In her last ten years Orozco received awards and recognition both inside Argentina and throughout Latin America. In 1972 and 1976 she travelled extensively in Europe. In 1986 she took part in the World Congress of poets. In 1998 she received the Juan Rulfo Prize for Latin American and Caribbean Literature, one of the most prestigious prizes in the Spanish-speaking world. During all this time she continued to write as her collection *Ultimos poemas* shows. "In the depths, the sun" and "It comes back with the rain" are among her very last poems, both marked by Orozco's desire to summon her earliest childhood and so evoke the sense of the entire trajectory of a life.

Uruguayan poet Marosa di Giorgio stands out as one of the most original poets of Latin America, creating a vast body of work remarkably consistent in style, tone and subject matter. From her first collection

Poemas published in 1953 to the full text of her last extensive work of poetry, *Diamelas a Clementina Médici*, published posthumously in 2008, she has written books of interconnected, untitled prose poems that blend aspects of her childhood on a small farm outside Salto with mythic, magic elements often marked by violence. The female speaking voice at each poem's centre is surrounded by threatening as well as protective presences. At times Di Giorgio's work reads as if it is about to become a novel but, instead of developing a story-line or a cast of characters, her prose poetry folds us in an a-temporal present where waves of sadness, terror, beauty and elation arise only to vanish. Her style is baroque in its fascination with repetitions, alliteration, plays on homophones and rhythmic cadences, as animals, plants, humans and mythic beings speak to each other, consume each other, copulate with each other. At times her work can recall Lautréamont or Michaux, at times Lewis Carrol or Kafka, but it always remains indelibly her own.

The child of Italian immigrants, Marosa di Giorgio grew up in the 1930's and 1940's on a small farm surrounded by gardens and orchards on the outskirts of the city of Salto, in northern Uruguay. Her poetry is marked by the rhythms of that life focussed on the cultivation and harvesting of orange groves, vineyards, olive trees, mulberry trees for silk worms, market gardens, and the stillness of nights that could be the Tuscan nights near the mountain village of Apua from where her father and maternal grandparents came. Like the moors in Emily Brontë's novel, the countryside around Salto provides the constant, almost claustrophobic shell of Marosa di Giorgio's often nightmarish, part supernatural sequences that always lead back to the one unresolvable life. Interestingly, in an interview with María Rosa Olivera-Williams, encouraged to cite influences, Marosa first countered by saying she had read so many people it was pointless to single out specific names and, in any case, she always went her own way, but she then named five "twin souls": Emily Dickinson, Emily Brontë[1], Edna Saint-Vincent Millay, Sylvia Plath and Uruguayan poet Concepción Silva Belinzon.

If Marosa di Giorgio grew up on a farm her parents were at the same time intensely interested in literature. Her childhood and adolescence were surrounded by books. As a child, rather like the young Emily Brontë, she constructed her own plays and later, from 1950 to 1968, was an actress with a professional company in Salto, performing in works by Federico García Lorca, Lope de Rueda, Clifford Odets, and Uruguayan playwright Florencio Sánchez, among many others. In 1986 she developed and performed a theatre piece using her own poems entitled *Diadema*. After opening in Montevideo she gave performances in Argentina, Mexico, Venezuela, the United States, Spain and France. If her work blurs the line between poetry and novel it also plays with the

1 Di Giorgio's *La liebre de marzo* (*The March Hare*) is also dedicated to Emily Brontë.

intersection of poetry and theatre. Her transformation of a selection of her poetry into a one-woman theatre piece suggests the dramatic quality of her work that, at one level, can be understood as a long monologue spoken by a character who both is and is not Marosa di Giorgio.

One problem facing the translator of Di Giorgio's work is the tension between the intricate, highly poetic qualities of individual passages and the overall architectural quality of each book and of the final single volume, *Los papeles salvajes*, published in 2008. Titles affix to books or sections of books, not to individual prose passages, so at one level we need to see each passage as like a panel of glass fitting into a large cathedral window. Each window in turn builds an inter-reflecting cathedral of glass. In an important way none of the individual prose poems she wrote is a stand-alone piece. Instead, the significant unit is, at its briefest, the titled section of the book or the whole book, but ultimately the whole opus. In those terms the present translation offers the reader two of the twenty-two magic glass windows that form the immense cathedral of *Los papeles salvajes*. At the same time, Marosa di Giorgio's work is intensely poetic at the level of individual sentences and prose poems, highlighting the repetition of sounds and rhythmic patterns. Much of that sound play inevitably disappears in translation. In a passage from "Funeral carriages laden with watermelons", for example, wordplay generates the sentence "Muchos pecaban en el pasto, otros pescaban en el pasto, ponían los anzuelos, y cazaban ratas . . ." ("Many sinned in the fields, others fished in the fields, they set out hooks and hunted rats . . .") The play between "pecaban" and "pescaban" disappears in English but at least the partial echo of alliteration is still there.

Di Giorgio's style as a writer is highly idiosyncratic. This extends to her use of punctuation, her abrupt shifts in tenses and the tendency for many passages to start as prose but, towards the end, employ line breaks to dramatize the poetic quality of the words. Disparate lists are a favourite lyric strategy where the everyday and the mysterious exist side by side. Equally, in a way that flouts the conventional injunction, in both English and Spanish, to avoid multiple adjectives, Di Giorgio loves lists of adjectives, often including superlatives like "hermossima", "bellissima". There are no authorial comments, morals drawn or flagged messages, but of its own nature her work invites both a feminist and a political reading. The descriptions of war breaking out, of violence and horror, inevitably call to mind the long period of military dictatorship in Uruguay from 1973 to 1985 with its death squads, kidnappings and torture. The writing itself privileges no one interpretation, just as the lists of plants, animals, visitors, presences and people, both real and invented, contain no hierarchies. Marosa's younger sister Nidia, her cousin Poupée, her father and mother, exist side by side with hares, bats, butterflies, hens, violets, lilies and roses endowed with extraordinary properties.

Likewise it is taken as a matter of course that the narrator remembers her life before she was born and at various moments starts flying. In her interview with Olivera-Williams, Marosa di Giorgio states: "All I tell and sing is my childhood in an agrarian zone, obscure, cut off and at the same time very free and iridescent . . . I saw Creation, Wonder, God's altar, inhabited by hares, lilies, teeth and corollas. Everything was there, everything will always be there."

The two sections of Di Giorgio's poetry presented here are the first and the second last sections respectively of her 1987 book *La falena* (*The Moth*). As well as poetry she published collections of short stories she called "erotic stories". In the last decades of her life Marosa di Giorgio travelled widely, giving readings at Universities and festivals in Argentina, Brazil, Chile, Paraguay, Mexico, Colombia, Spain, and the United States, while collections of her short stories appeared in Latin America and France. She was awarded a range of prizes for her poetry both in Uruguay and internationally. Over the last few years her work has slowly begun to appear in English translations, largely due to the work of Jeannine Pitas, Adam Gianelli, and Kathryn Kopple. Nevertheless, including the translations published by Vagabond, less than a third of her poetry is available in English. After a long treatment for bone cancer, first diagnosed in 1993, Marosa di Giorgio died in Montevideo in 2004.

Born in Montevideo in 1961, Jorge Palma lived

his late teens and twenties under Uruguay's military dictatorship. His poetry is marked by the desire to communicate and to respond to the social-political world around him. His first collection of poems *Entre el viento y la sombra* was published in 1989 and has been followed by five further books of poetry as well as a collection of short stories, *Paraísos artificiales*. In an interview conducted by email in late 2015, Palma describes his earliest poetry as arising from images that transformed into words and lines. Among the first poets he read were Antonio Machado, Miguel Hernández, Vicente Aleixandre, Pound and Neruda. Also influential were Eliot, Vallejo and Apollinaire. However, it was fellow Uruguayan Mario Benedetti, the Argentine Gonzales Tuñón and Brazilian Ferreira Gullar whose work he cites as most influential in the development of his poetry, confirming for him the value of what could be achieved in an everyday, straight-talking style. As if to make the point in a different way Palma indicates his preference for the working-class realistic voice of Cesare Pavese over the more refined, elliptical style of Eugenio Montale. In the interview Palma writes, "There is much self-referential poetry, very dedicated to looking into oneself. Everything has its validity. But I prefer poetry where you feel, hear, 'smell' life. Therefore Gelman, Benedetti, Vallejo, Zurita, Kozer, Parra, Cardenal, Gullar . . .". In itself this is a very varied list, including poets – Cuban José Kozer and Chilean Raúl Zurita – considered neo-baroque as well as the older inventor of "anti-poetry" Nicanor Parra, alongside more obviously political poets, as well as the great Peruvian poet César Vallejo, himself a master of many styles.

In many ways representative of Palma's poetry "Paraphernalia", from his 2006 collection *La vía lactea*, is both the poem of an individual and a vehicle of social-political reflection. Topical but in no way predictable, shifting and restless, it moves rapidly from image to image to arrive at the surprise of the last line. At times, as in the fourth stanza, the images gather in baroque profusion to suggest an apocalyptic wasteland, but the poem does not settle there or in any one place till its conclusion. The pigeon with "its bloodied beak" bringing to the everyday table "a slap from the world" is itself perhaps a victim as well, but the last line – as often in Palma's poetry – focuses on all the speaker does not know. Part of the fascination of an overtly political poem like "The working class don't go to paradise" is the way it sidesteps traditional rhetoric, whether of left or right, to offer a nuanced, and far bleaker, view of our world. Satirical humour, perhaps reminiscent of Chilean poet Nicanor Parra, can be seen in "Salaries", yet Palma is also willing to risk the very open statement of a personal vision of social ethics, charged with fundamental optimism, in "Immortals". There are also poems of intimate affection, of self-exposure, like "Child and leopard". It may well be that for Jorge Palma, as for many of his generation who grew up in a world of violent political repression, life and poetry seem much too precious for excessive introspection or for any poetics that, whether from fear of being labelled sentimental or the desire to seem "new", leads away from an immediate engagement with life.

Jorge Palma has presented his poetry at festivals in Nicaragua and Macedonia – which is where in 2009 I had the good fortune to meet him and discover his poetry – and a selection of his poems was included in the Spanish anthology of world poetry *Aldea poética* (1997). This is the first selection of his poems translated into English. In general the gap between the poetry written in Latin America and the amount available in English translation is staggering. Apart from Neruda, Vallejo and Octavio Paz, only a handful of other poets – not necessarily the best or most important – have a significant proportion of their work available in English. For Marosa di Giorgio it is less than a third. With Olga Orozco even less is available. Of a total of 192 poems in Orozco's *Poesía completa* Mary Crow's selection, *Engravings torn from Insomnia*, contains only 23 poems and there are 18 further poems translated in the present book. Other extraordinarily under-translated Latin American poets would include Mexican Gerardo Deniz, Argentine Néstor Perlongher, Cuban Gastón Baquero and Uruguayan Eduardo Espina, to name just a very few. This present selection aims in some small measure to address that gap.

Peter Boyle

NOTES

Extracts from an interview with Olga Orozco are from Jacobo Sefamí, *De la imaginación poética*, São Paulo: Lumme, 2013. María Rosa Olivera-William's interview with Marosa di Giorgio is contained in her article "La imaginación salvaje: Marosa di Giorgio", *Revista Iberoamericana*, 71: 211, Abril-Junio 2005. The translations are my own. The information given about Marosa di Giorgio's life is based on the Biographic Summary by Daniel García Helder provided in *Los papeles salvajes*. I am also indebted to the comments provided by Adam Gianelli in his Introduction to *Diadema* and to Roberto Echavarren's article "Marosa di Giorgio, Última poeta de Uruguay", *Revista Iberoamericana* (available online).

The Spanish originals for the translations of Orozco and Di Giorgio are from: Olga Orozco, *Poesía completa*, Buenos Aires: Adriana Hidalgo, 2012, and Marosa di Giorgio, *Los papeles salvajes*, Buenos Aires: Adriana Hidalgo, 2008. Jorge Palma's poems are selected from *La via lactea* (Montevideo: Trilce, 2006) and *Lugar de las utopías* (Montevideo: Trilce, 2007).

Details of previous translations into English of Orozco and Di Giorgio are as follows: Olga Orozco, *Engravings torn from Insomnia*, Translations by Mary Crow. Rochester: BOA, 2002. Marosa di Giorgio, *The March Hare*, Translated by Kathryn Kopple. Kindle Edition, 2013. Marosa di Giorgio, *Diadem*, Translations by Adam Gianelli. Rochester: BOA, 2012. Marosa di Giorgio, *The History of Violets*, Translated by Jeannine Pitas. Brooklyn: Ugly Duckling Press, 2010.

OLGA OROZCO

CARTOMANCY

The dogs that sniff out the lineage of ghosts,
listen to them barking,
listen to them tear apart the cloth of the omen.
Listen. Someone approaches:
the floorboards are creaking under your feet
as if you'll never stop fleeing, never stop arriving.
You seal the doors with your name written
    in the ashes of the past and the future.
But someone has come.
And other faces have breathed your face's image off all
    the mirrors
and you're nothing more than a candle that's torn apart,
an underwater moon invaded by struggles and triumphs,
    by ferns.

Here lies what is, what was, what will come, what may come.
You have seven answers for seven questions.
Your card which is the sign of the World shows this:
on your right the Angel,
on your left the Demon.

Who is calling? Who is calling from your birth all the way
    to your death,
with a broken key, with a ring buried years ago?
What creatures are gliding above their own footsteps like
    a flock of birds?

The Stars light up the enigmatic sky.
Yet what you want to see can't be looked at face to face:
its light belongs to a different kingdom.
And it's still not the hour. And there will be time.

Better to decipher the name of the one who enters.
His card is the Madman's with his patient net for
    catching butterflies.
He is the eternal guest.
He is the imagined Emperor of the world who lives
    inside you.
Don't ask who he is. You know him
for you've looked for him under every stone and in every
    abyss.
The two of you sat up together waiting for the arrival of
    a miracle:
a poem where everything would be all of this and also
    you –
something more than all of this –
But nothing has come.
Nothing that's any more than these sterile words.
And maybe it's too late now.

Let us see who is seated here.
The woman who is wrapped in linen and caws
while she weaves and unweaves your shirt
has the black butterfly for a heart.
Yet your life is long; its chord will break far, very far from
    here.

I read it in the sands of the Moon where the journey is written,
where the house is drawn where you drown like a pale
    stretch mark
in the night spun from great spider-webs by your Death,
    the spinner of your thread.
Yet beware of water, love and fire.

Beware of love, the one thing that remains.
For today, for tomorrow, for after tomorrow.
Beware for it shines with the dazzling light of tears and swords.
Its glory is the Sun's, just as much as its furies and its pride.
But you will never know peace
for your Strength is the strength of storms and Restraint
    weeps, its face to the wall.
You will never sleep side by side with happiness
for in all your steps is an edge of grief that foretells crime
    or farewells,
and the Hanged Man announces to me
the terrifying night that is your destiny.

Do you want to know who loves you?
The one stepping out to meet me comes from your own heart.
Masks of mud are shining on his face; under his skin
flows the pale shadow of every solitary watcher.
In his one life he is here to live a procession of lives and deaths.
He came to learn horses, trees, stones
and was left weeping over every shameful act.
You have raised a wall to protect him
but he never wanted the Tower that now surrounds him,

the silk prison where love jangles the keys of an
    incorruptible jailer.
Meanwhile the Cart waits for the signal to leave:
day's appearance in the clothing of the Hermit.
But it's still not time to turn your blood into the stone of
    memory.
The two of you lie there still in the constellation of the
    Lovers,
that river of fire that flows by consuming time's belt
as it consumes you,
and I dare say you both belong to a race of shipwrecked
    mariners
who drown without salvation or any breath of hope.

Now cover yourself with the breastplate of power or
    forgiveness, as if you knew no fear,
for I'm going to show you the one who hates you.
Don't you hear her heart beating like a darkened wing?
Like me, can't you see her brush your side with a fistful
    of frost?
It's her, the Empress of all your broken homes,
she who casts your image in wax for the ritual sacrifices,
who buries a dove in the shadows so the air in your house
    will grow dark,
who blocks your steps with branches from a dead tree,
    with shrunken fingernails, with words.
She hasn't always been the same woman, but whoever
    she may be it's her
for her power lies simply in this: to be other than you.

That is her spell.

Though the Conjuror may roll the dice on the table of
destiny

and your enemy knots your name thrice on a hostile rope,

at least five of us know the game is useless,

the triumph no triumph –

only the luckless man's sceptre given to him by the
homeless King,

a boneyard of dreams where the ghost of the lover who
refuses to die goes on wandering.

You will stay in darkness, you will stay alone.

You will stay exposed to the heart's wild rages, ready to
wound the one who kills you.

Don't invoke Justice. The serpent has taken refuge on its
empty throne.

Don't try and find your talisman of fish-bones

for the night is long and your hangmen are many.

Since dawn their purple blood has muddied your threshold,

has marked your door with the three ill-omened signs

in spades, in hearts, in clubs.

Cruelty has locked you inside a circle of spades.

With the two of gold coins, eyelids coated in flaking scales
have cunningly annihilated you.

Violence has traced a blue lightning bolt on your throat
with its wand of clubs.

And meanwhile they stretch out the mat of burning coals
for you.

And now the Kings have arrived.

They come to fulfil the prophecy.

They come to inhabit the three shadows of death that
    will accompany your own death

until the Wheel of Destiny spins no more.

GENESIS

Time wears no sign on its skin.
Nothing. Not the sudden winter carpet that predicts jagged
    slashes of lightning maybe even tomorrow.
Nor those fires that have been here forever, announcing
    a torch that will glow in the waters of all the future.
Not even the warning tremor underneath a sigh from the
    abyss that flows out into never or yesterday.
Nothing. No promised land.
Only a quicklime desert as black as white,
an eager ghost born from rocks to gnaw on the millennia's
    sleep,
the outward fall which is the sleep with which the rocks sleep.
No one. Only the echo of footsteps and no one going away,
and a confused bed on the march towards the finish line.

I was lying there:
I with my eyes wide open.
In each hand I had a cave to look at God,
and a trail of ants was walking from his shadow to my heart
    and my head.

And in the sky someone shattered the grey earthenware jar
    where
they go up to drink memories;
then they ripped apart the record of blind, treacherously
    wounded oaths

and destroyed the tablets of the law written in the congealed
blood of dead histories.
Someone made a bonfire and one by one threw in the
fragments.
The sky was burning as it extinguished every hell
and, on earth, their traces, all evidence, was wiped out.
I was suspended in some time of holy expiation.
I was in some very clear-seeing part of God;
I with my eyes shut tight.

Then they pronounced the word.

There was a loud cry of green paradise that rises and rips up
the roots of stone,
and its heavenly prow moved forward between light and
darkness.
They opened the floodgates.
A vast dazzling wave filled the hollow of every still
uninhabited hope,
and on their upward surface the waters had the colour of a
mirror in
which no one has ever looked at themselves
and, beneath, the brilliance of a stormy cave that looks out
forever for the first time.
Suddenly the waters drew back.
A land arose to inscribe in fire every step of the future,
to wrap the fall and each birth's reversal in thirsty grass,
to place once more, locked in each heart, the kernel of
mystery.

They lifted the seals.

The jail of the great day opened its doors to the sun's
    delirium

on condition that each new imprisonment of time dazzle
    the eyes,

on condition that every night and its veil of revelation fall at
    the moon's feet.

They sowed in the waters and on the winds.

And from that moment there was a single shadow drowned
    in a thousand shadows,

a single unnamed glow in the tiered light that illuminates
    the ladder of dreams to its end.

And from that moment an edge of burning feathers stretched
    from the most remote distances,

wings arriving and leaving in a flight to say goodbye to all
    goodbyes.

The wings stirred up a deep sigh in the bowels of all of space.

It brushed the deepest ocean floor of the blood;

it was stamens shivering in the vertigo of the air;

and the soul descended to the luminous mud to take on
    that shape

that would match its own image,

and the flesh rose up as a perfect number,

as the promised difference between the beginning and
    the end.

Then evening and morning were fulfilled
on the last day of the centuries.

I was facing you;
I with my eyes wide open under your eyes
in the first dawn of oblivion.

FOR EMILIO IN HIS HEAVEN

Here are your keepsakes:
this mild blight of violets
falling uselessly on forgotten days and hours;
your name,
the persistent name your hand left behind on stones;
the familiar tree, its sound always green against the
    windowpane;
my childhood, so close,
in the same garden where the grass still grows,
where your head so often would suddenly
rest beside me in the thickets of darkness.

Everything's still the same.
When, like now, standing at the far wall we call each
    other again:
everything's still the same.
Here, pale adolescent, lies your territory:
damp grassland for your clandestine feet,
the sour taste of thistles, familiar frost at daybreak,
old old stories,
the earth where we were born, an identical mist hovering
    over our tears.

– Do you remember snow falling? So long ago now.
How your hair's grown since then!
And yet you still wear its ephemeral flowers on your skin

and your forehead bends under the very same sky
so bright and dazzling.

Why, like a god to his world, do you have to come back
    bringing a landscape I loved?
Do you still remember snow falling?

How alone your dwelling place would be today,
its iron bars and flowers behind useless walls!

Left behind, its youth resembles your body,
now it will miss your too obstinate silences,
your skin, as desolate as a country only visited by
    ash-grey petals
that have watched, for so long now, the inexhaustible
    patience of ants
going back and forth through their lonely ruins.

Wait, wait, my darling:
that's not the cold face of the terrifying snow, not the face
of last night's dream.
Listen once more, my darling, just once more:
the sand's unmistakeable scratching on the fence,
grandmother's cry,
the same loneliness, its absolute truth,
and this long future: staring at our hands till they grow old.

CANTOS TO BERENICE (V)

You reigned in Bubastis
your feet in earth, like the Nile,
a constellation for a headdress above your heavenly double.
You were the Sun's daughter and fought against night's
    malevolent ones –
mire, treason or mole, rodents gnawing at the house wall, at
    the bed of lovemaking –
from the bejewelled dynasties of stone
to ash-laden kitchen spices, multiplying yourself,
from the temple's halo to the steam off cooking pots.
Solitary sphinx or domestic sybil,
you were the goddess Lar and in every fold, every brushy patch
of your inexplicable anatomy, you housed a god, like some
    insomniac flea.
Through the ears of Isis or Osiris you discovered
that your names were Bastet and Bast and that other name
    only you know
(or maybe a cat doesn't need three names?)
but when the Furies nibbled away at your heart like a
    honeycomb of plagues
you puffed yourself up till you claimed kinship with the lion,
then you were called Sekhet, the revenger.
But the gods, the gods too die to be immortal
and, once again, any day they like, burn dust and garbage.
Your little bell rolled round, its music silenced by the wind.
Your little pouch lies scattered among countless mouths of sand.

And now your shield is a blurred idol for lizards and
    centipedes.
The centuries have bound and wrapped you in your
    wasted necropolis –
that city swathed in bandages that walks through
    children's nightmares –
and because each body by itself is one small part
of the immense sarcophagus of a god
you were hardly even you and, at the same time, a legion
    sitting in suspense,
seated there, you with that air
of being always at ready, sitting on guard
at the threshold.

CANTOS TO BERENICE (VI)

You didn't eat the lotus of oblivion –
the Homeric privilege of the gods –
already you knew whoever forgets becomes an inanimate
      object –
mere driftwood or floating debris –
whatever the capricious sea wants to do with someone's
      memories.
And so one day you excavated your garbage mound of
      frozen ghosts
and tied together once more with tender threads tiny
      scattered bones,
woven fabrics in love with the smell of rain,
viscera sweet as supernatural honeycombs for the queen bee,
teeth that were wolves on the steppes of the moon,
claws that were tigers in the deep embalmed forest.
And you wrapped it all in that sack of star-bright coal
that you tossed over here, as if to a moving train,
the sack with a hole somewhere through which they
      breathe you in,
to which you must return.

CANTOS TO BERENICE (VII)

You still conserve intact, with perfect memory,
the mark of an ancient sacrament under your palate:
your stamp of being chosen, your dark full moon,
black salt of the black scarab with which they baptised
    your sacred lineage,
that doubtless you wear from one pilgrimage to another.
For whom these instructions?
What did you leave here? What possessions?
What millennial mistake did you come back to correct?
Now you come walking backwards like those who have
    seen.
You draw back towards gates that fly away like wandering
    birds.
Maybe you're startled by the unseen hand with which
    they try to hold onto you
or else you're scared off by that hollow imitation of
    another hand
you thought you'd meet there.
You knock over the plate and stay mute like those who
    return,
like those who know life is a gagged absence,
and silence
a knitted-up mouth feigning oblivion.

CANTOS TO BERENICE (IX)

But leap, leap one more time over the poppies,
leap over the June bonfires and don't get burnt
as if you knew how to do that.
Gaze once more at the full moon with your half open shadow
though we do nothing but spread like drifting fog,
like an invasion of transparent spiders,
the suspicion that we are again witch and messenger.
Two yellow dogs won't lick your traces,
you won't fly on goosebumps of clouds to the party on the
    Brocken.
The only owl we had was our alert wakefulness in
    the depths of sleep,
the only footman-frog a cold gust of wind to chase away
    the spirits.
Our accursed pact with the devil
was our power of terror against the uncatchable rodents
who would dig out their traps under the house;
our satanic sign,
the same excess in the pupil
to hasten there the intentions of muffled night;
our pact in blood,
nothing more than the exchange of insoluble enigmas:
other versions of our very selves.

CANTOS TO BERENICE (XIV)

You used to play at hiding among the kitchen utensils
like a strange wild object among inexplicable exotica
or at disappearing into the complicit foliage
with the cloak of some sleeping dryad under evening's
     veils
or you were the stiff matter in a sheet of paper that floats
     up and leaves.
You would fill the cupboards with small quivering things
or populate empty dresses with decapitated creatures and
     ghosts.
You were bird and cricket, blind moss and wandering
     topazes.
Now I know you were trying to put your pursuer off the
     scent
with your constantly changing masks.
The tunnel with a hare's ears and that chasing
of invisible night butterflies weren't lies after all.
It was just that I didn't know how to cover your tracks.
Little by little your enemy drew close
and wrapped you in his webs like a cloak of sodden rags.
You emerged the victor in the irreversible game of not
     being.
Nevertheless, even now, a certain breathing
glides over a cold pane of glass at my back.
And then there's that shining insect among the flowers,
the inexplicable disappearance of small things,

night after night a creature's ghostly nose pressing against
the window,
I don't know, it could be,
who's to guarantee you're not playing at being here,
pretending to be caught?

CANTOS TO BERENICE (XVII)

Though all our traces may be wiped clean just like
    candles at dawn
and you maybe can't remember backwards, like the
    White Queen,
leave me your smile in the air.
Perhaps by now you're as immense as all my dead,
with your skin night after night hiding the overflowing
    night of farewell:
one eye on Achernar, the other on Sirius,
your ears stuck to the deafening wall of other planets,
your vast body drowned in their boiling ablution,
in their Jordan of stars.
Maybe my head would be impossible, my voice not even
    a void,
my words less than tattered rags of some ridiculous
    language.
But leave me your smile in the air:
a gentle vibration to coat in quicksilver a sliver of the
    glass of absence,
that brief vigil tattooed in live flame in a corner,
a tender sign to perforate one by one the leaves of that
    harsh calendar of snow.
Leave me your smile
as some form of perpetual guardian,
Berenice.

MASKS DOUBLING EVERYONE

Far off,
leaping from heart to heart,
beyond the crown of mist that breathes me from the depths
    of vertigo,
I hear the drum roll with which they summon me to the land
    of no one.
(Who stands up inside me?
Who rises from the honoured seat of their death, from their
    mat of blackberries
and walks with the memory of my feet?)
I abandon my body to itself like a suit of armour against
    exposure to the inner elements
and lay down my name like a weapon only fit to wound.
(Where to go to find
the moon's ecstasy against the windows of all places of shelter?)
With different hands I open the gate to the path that leads
    I don't know where
and go forward into the night of strangers.
(Where did the day take my sign,
pale in its isolation,
trace of an insignia my poor victory snatched from time?)
Through different eyes I look at this wall of mist
where one by one all have marked the hieroglyph of their
    loneliness in blood,
loosed their moorings, sailed off into shipwreck with a ghost
    boat's farewell.

(Wasn't there far off, some other place, other time,
a foreign land,
a race of all but one, called the race of the others,
a language of the blind that made its way upwards
through bubbling sounds, buzzing noises
towards the deafness of night?)
On the inside of everyone only a resting place under
     a frieze of masks;
inside everyone a single effigy inscribed on the soul's
     reverse side;
inside everyone each story takes place everywhere;
there's no death that doesn't kill,
no birth that's foreign, no uninhabited love.
(Weren't we hostages of a fall,
a rain of stones unstuck from the sky,
a trickle of insects trying to cross the punishing bonfire?)
Any man is the darkened version of a Great King
     wounded in his side.

In each dream I wake with the dream that Someone is
     dreaming the world.
It is God's eve.
He is joining his bits and pieces together in us.

BETWEEN DOG AND WOLF

They seal me off inside myself.
They divide me in two.
Each day they give birth to me as both patience
and a black organism that roars like the sea.
Later they trim me with the scissors of nightmare
and I fall into this world, my blood split between my two
    sides:
one side worked over by the fangs of a lonely fury,
the other dissolving in the mist of the great herds.
I've no way to know who's the boss here.
I change under my skin from dog to wolf.
I decree the plague and, with both sides of my body on fire,
    cross the plains of the future and the past;
I lie down to gnaw the tender bones of all those
    dead dreams in the sky-blue meadows.
My kingdom lies in my shadow and travels with me
    wherever I go
or collapses in ruins, its gates open to the enemy's invasion.
Every night with my teeth I rip apart any knot that's tied to
    the heart
and each dawn I wake up, the cage of obedience on my back.
If I devour my god I wear his face under my mask,
and yet, in the watering trough of men, I drink only
    compassion's velvety poison and it scrapes my guts.
I've embroidered the tourney in the two weaves of
    the tapestry:

I've won my beast's sceptre out in the wind and the rain,
and awarded rags of meekness as trophy.
But, inside me, who wins?
Who defends my solitary bastion in the wilderness, my
    shroud of sleep?
And who slowly, wrapped in darkness, is gnawing my lips
    using my own teeth?

"PAVANE FOR A DEAD PRINCESS"

for Alejandra Pizarnik

Little sentry guard,
you fall once again through the fissure of night
armed with nothing but your open eyes and terror
against the insoluble invaders of the blank page.
They were legion.
Legion made flesh was their name
and they multiplied the more you unpicked the fabric
    till the very last thread,
cowering in your corner against the voracious spiderwebs
    of nothingness.
Closing your eyes means becoming the dwelling place
    of the whole universe.
Open them and you draw the boundary line and you stay
    out there at the mercy of the sky.
To walk on that line is to lose your place.
Bouts of insomnia like long tunnels for testing every
    reality's inconsistency;
nights and more nights perforated by a single bullet that
    nails you into the dark,
the same attempt to recognise yourself on waking inside
    the memory of death:
that perverse temptation,
that adorable angel with a pig's snout.
Who spoke of spells to counteract the wound of one's birth?

Who mentioned bribes for the emissaries of one's future?
Only there was a garden: in the depths of everything there
    is a garden
where the blue flower from Novalis' dream opens.
Cruel flower, vampire flower,
more treacherous than the trap hidden in the plush of the wall,
a flower you can never reach without leaving your head or
    whatever blood you still have on the threshold.
But, not caring, you kept leaning over to pick it, with no
    foothold,
just inward abysses.
You planned to swap it for the starving creature who was
    taking over your house.
You built little ravenous castles in her honour;
you wore feathers that had broken free from the bonfire of
    every possible paradise;
you trained small dangerous animals to gnaw away the
    bridges of salvation;
you lost yourself just like the beggar woman with her
    delusion of wolves;
you tried out languages like acids, like tentacles,
like ropes in the hands of a strangler.
Ah what poetry does, cutting your veins with dawn's sharp
    edge,
and those bloodless lips sucking down venoms as speech
    turns empty.
And suddenly there's no more.
The flasks have shattered.
Lights and pencils cracked in splinters.

The paper was torn apart with a tear down which you
    glide into one more labyrinth.
All the doors are for getting out.
And everything is at the back of mirrors.
Little traveller,
alone with your collection box of visions
and the same unbearable sense of abandonment under
    your feet:
clearly with your voices you're calling out like a drowned
    woman for passage across;
clearly your enormous shadow that continues to fly above
    you in the search for another still holds you back,
or you meet an insect whose membranes hide all chaos
    and you tremble,
or you're frightened by the sea that, so you think, fits into
    this single tear.
But now that the silence has wrapped you twice over in
    its wings like a mantle
I tell you again:
in the depths of everything there is a garden.
Your garden is there.
Talitha cumi.

MUTATIONS OF REALITY

Rose, oh the pure contradiction,
delight of being nobody's sleep
under so many lids
Rainer Maria Rilke

The way damp rock holds no water
and the reflection in the glass can't translate the scene at
    the garden's centre?
The way my shadow neither precedes nor follows me but
    simply testifies by its light
and a phosphorescent bone doesn't walk off in search of
    scattered ashes
for the feast day of the resurrection?

Maybe, or like any wonder stripped bare by the hands of
    the law.

I don't deny reality has no more powers and less cracks
than an iron breastplate binding the condensations of
    sleep and night
or a drop of wax sealing our eyesight with abysses and
    paradises
half-opening like a secret panel
through the workings of a spell or a mistake.

But reality's just a sedentary longing, like wanting to tie
    the moon to each door;

nothing more than an attempt to push back those vague
   frontiers
that switch places –
to where? to when? –
or forever emigrate, breathed out suddenly by the flight of
   some impenetrable revelation.

I know that in every way reality's nomadic,
as suspect, as ambiguous as my own anatomy.

I'm saying she too got here through some wild leap in the dark
and, like me, keeps
nostalgias and fears of fauna and flora
like those Hieronymus Bosch transplanted from the scourings
   of chaos,
clouds sticky-taped over the scars of mutilations,
vertigos resembling an exodus of stars,
roots so deep they sometimes shake the pillars of what was
   the floor
and then scream their deafening claim to another world.

Like me a captive, with constellations and ants,
perhaps inside a glass ball where souls wander,
I've seen reality shrink and take the form of puny Jonah
   inside the whale
or endlessly expand into that skin which, in a stream of
   vapour, breathes out all the sky:
indissoluble stowaway groping through the bilge water of the
   unknown

or all-encompassing beast at the moment of exploding
    against the wire fence around limbo.
And neither the narrow nor the immeasurably broad gate
    offered a way out.

Like me, protector of one of destiny's indecipherable masks,
reality dresses up as a witch and with a sigh transforms
    dazzling birds to legions of rats,
or puts all of yesterday's and tomorrow's wine in a pot to
    evaporate
till all that's left in the bottom are bitter dregs that
    accentuate thirst
with their taste of never or nostalgia;
or she turns into a Queen and tries on the clothes of some
    impossible beauty,
stuffed toys studded with distance,
that are bandages of oblivion,
rags of a beggar woman banging her face against my window
or a miser's nudity as, into my jewelry box, she pours her
    treasures gnawed by leprosy.
And we will never understand our true role in the story.

A stranger, like me, to the chaotic ties that unite us
and bind my neck with knots of rebellion, suspicion,
    astonishment,
sometimes she stares at me as absorbed as if we had never
    known each other
and takes her pillow from under my feet till I lose sight of
    her wing-beats,

when she doesn't press close with a murderous stare, pinning
me against my precipices
to despoil me with her hands of asphyxia and insanity;
or maybe suddenly, in the blink of an eye, she'll take on a
quite different appearance?
dye my walls in mourning?
swap objects, storms, groves of trees about, just to get me lost?
And with barely a moment of peace between us.

Precarious, like me,
here, where we are barely a pale transcription of absence,
she multiplies herself into regions that mirror the fires of lost
memory,
opens cracks in surfaces like blind slashes to extract the future,
with her starving dogs she sniffs out each omen that flees
with death
and from mutation to mutation she chases glimmers that
shatter into hallucinations.
And she ends up grasping nothing more than spectres of the
unknown images she reflects.
You grasp no more yourself,
though in all the glitter you deny your true task and bury it
in the rubble;
though you trace your limits and abide by the knife of the
narrow law;
however much you tear away all your layers to show
that the rose of Rilke seals no sleep under so many lids.

THE SUBMERGED CONTINENT

Matchless head,
only half visible wherever it's seen from,
half rescued from endless exile inside the fog-filled head.
Opaque from the outside,
impermeable to baptism by light,
porous as a sponge to the distillations of indissoluble night.
Yet it shines inwardly;
it is burning in a whirlwind of crystals,
of sparks broken loose from sleep's furnace,
of a blue vertigo that testifies this is the sky's tomb.
Supposedly at some time it was a part broken loose from
     God,
in the guise of darkness,
and it tumbled downwards, cut off by the serpent's
     damnation.
No one knows the millennia, the metamorphosis,
the stupefying layers of groundwater it had to cross
     to reach here,
spinning through roots like a mole's shadow,
moving forward next like a blind planet
condensed to smoke, to vapour, to eclipse.
It was breathed upwards,
erected at the top of a floating trunk that barely holds onto
     it,
with two deaf caverns to hear the voice that breaks against
     the wall,

with two hollow grooves to see the fall from a cloister,
with the smell of a beast trapped under the skin,
tasting like buried bread during a fast,
with that insatiable tongue
that consumes the language of the dead in great bursts
    of flame.
Head filled with storms,
undecipherable head,
head lost in thought:
you're like some circular hell
where the persecutor suddenly becomes the persecuted,
always behind yourself, or in front of me,
who doesn't know where I spring from sometimes,
    grasped by the neck
but not finding the knots that tie me to this strange head.

INTERROGATION OF THE BIRD THROUGH ITS SONG

In some eyes you see the indigo dregs left by twilights
     as they fade –
a wing that remains, a shadow of absence.
Such eyes are made to distinguish even the very last
     trace of melancholy,
to see in the rain an inventory of lost blessings
just as an inner winter is needed
"to behold the frost and the junipers shagged with ice"
Wallace Stevens said, freezing the ears and the eye's pupil,
turned maybe into the snowman who contemplates the
     nothing with the nothing
and who hears only the wind
with no gospel that mightn't be the unique sound of
     the wind
(though maybe it will speak of the greatest possible
     bareness, not clarity).
But I know that everything dark is only explored using
     the night I have,
that the rock half opens before the rock
in the same way as the heart is weighed with its abyss.
Is there any other way of peering right down to the
     deepest subsoil,
to the depths of another wound, of another hell?
There's no other lamp for examining what's close,
     what's strange, what's distant.

It's shown by the elusive meaning of the rat's squeal
    between its glass walls,
as it slips on the ladder of some inconceivable light;
the star proclaims it with its distant code that's tied
    to a certain trembling,
maybe to someone's death, someone already gone;
it's confirmed by the I that walks with you and is memory
    wherever you forget,
and by that vast glittering other
that emerges for a meeting under the water of
    transformations,
and sometimes isn't person or colour, or perfume or any
    trace of this world.
Both are spun from the exact substance of silence.
They resemble God in his version as reversible guest:
the soul that inhabits you is also the gaze of the sky that
    includes you.

ANIMAL THAT BREATHES

To breathe in and breathe out. Such is the strategy in this mutual transfusion with the whole universe.

Day and night, like two spongy organisms glued to the wall of the visible by this double rise and fall of the breath that upholds the cosmogonies in mid-air, we expand and contract, the universe and I. On my side I take it in as blue sky, I exhale it as an excreta of mist and then once more breathe it in. In its turn it incorporates me into the whole mechanism, then expels me into that alien wild element which is my own, the threshold's sharp edge, and then once again it breathes me in. We survive together at the same distance, body against body, one in favour of the other, one at the expense of the other – something more than witnesses – just as in a siege, just as in certain plants, just as in the secret, like with Adam and God.

Who would pretend to be the winner here? One mistake would be enough for our fates to be swapped for the gliding of a feather across the immense void. My pride is so focussed on the clarity of its wild devotion, on my unequal side of the coin – so weak and doubtless essential – it swells in proportion to its smallness.

I fulfil my role. Like a cautious polyp I preserve my modest place. With great difficulty I stand on tiptoe on some windowsill to find a level of exchange appropriate for low flying, a point where I might relinquish my own construction with dignity.

Weaker than my eyes, faster than my hands, further off than the gesture of another face, this wrong-headed nose that suddenly strips me of the smooth patience of my skin and hurls me into the world of others, always unknown, always the outsider.

And nevertheless it precedes me. It cloaks me with apparent solidity, ideally rock-like, and then lays me bare to the winds that invade over a few precarious, vulnerable ditches scarcely defended in trembling and suspicion.

And so, with no further ado, poking my nose into old habits and dangers, glued like a dog to the heels of the future, I pile up cloud-like ghosts, haloes instead of blessings, the useless fluff accumulated in nostalgic ports, in floating cities that threaten to return, in gardens smelling of the crazed memory of a promised paradise.

Ah, lethargic perfumes, traces left by rain and bodies, trails of breath that, like some asphyxiating rope, coil round the throat of my future.

Little by little a volatile alchemy builds up in the cracks, evaporating the years' hardened condensations. It digs me out and suffocates me, breathes me out in great clear breaths that are the bloodless form of my final skeleton.

And though the mutual transfusion with the whole universe goes on, I know that "there, in that place, in the dark moss I am mortal, and in my dreams a beast's snout sniffs endlessly", a relentless snout drawing the breath out of me, right to the very last stench.

IN THE DEPTHS, THE SUN

Do you need to reach the very bottom of the cup to see
    your destiny?
Here there's an explosion of stars, two birds flying, a
    broken ring,
and something resembling a shadow, standing, beside
    a lamp.
All scattered over a white desert, a desert of snow,
    indecipherable.
Maybe they are simply illegible fragments of days
    already lived,
portions of a story torn apart by time's merciless teeth.

But from very early I saw my future in a cloud,
or in that glass bubble
where there was a wandering house with its fairytale
    party lights
and a magic garden that it suddenly bore very far away –
always, in the depths of everything there is a garden –
as far as the hidden gate that leads to all dangers and the
    immense unknown,
to come back, timid or dazzled, and enter my indifferent
    refuge, my velvet paradise.
                    How bright the sun was shining then!

A few years later I discovered my sentence
inscribed on the dark reverse side of a rock that rolled
    along with the wind
from my journey's end to its very beginning.
It was my punishment, my fiery mandate,
to find God's secret writing scattered among the images of
    the world,
under the grass, in the lightning flash, in memories of rain.
The impossible attempt to thread the signs together,
the ciphered alphabet that begins in the Word and ends in
    my bones.
        Always, above each syllable, the sun was burning!

Through many years I read more than once the depths of
    my fate –
heaven and hell mixed together –
I read this in eyes full of sparks and dark shadows,
eyes for gazing as into the long insomnia of deep waters –
ah, but how different what I saw in those waters from what
    I'd seen through tears.
In them I saw myself as the most intense eternal spring,
though always sucked up by whirlwinds, by vertigo at
    the abyss' edge.
Till night grew heavy around me,
till the waters closed over.
        And till then the sun blinded as never before!

Now I'm alone, my watchful shadow facing the wall,
staring into the last sign my destiny has traced
    everywhere:
a wide crack that runs like a river, like a black pit, a sheer
    drop.
Though maybe it's not a frontier,
no uncrossable gulf between my visible yesterday and
    my blind tomorrow,
but just the mark of union between the brief earth and
    the promised kingdom.
                    And the sun? The sun now no more?

If you keep looking into the depths of the cup you will
    never see the sun of the other side,
from here you will never see anything,
you will see no beyond – just a white desert.

IT COMES BACK WHEN THE RAIN

Sisters of air and cold, my sisters:
what is that song which continues along the branches and
    rolls against the window?
What is that song I've lost that's spinning in the wind
and still comes back?
It's far away, very far,
among the first dawns of a garden watched over by angels
    and nettles,
a paradise where there's no darkness, no forgetting.
We used to sing that song for ever and ever.
We used to sing a bond holding us together till after the world.
That was a long time ago, sister of silence and moon.
It was in your adolescence, in my most affectionate childhood,
when you'd barely peeked at the sinuous waters of love
that soon enough pulled you under,
when against our straight-forwardness you still dressed in a
    sampler of apparitions:
ghost bride, soul in pain or mad beggar woman;
but the next day you were peace and the light brushing of
    grass-blades.
When you left, the song lost its blue stained-glass window.
That was long ago, sister of escapades and sunshine.
I was the smallest and followed your footsteps through
    magic places

where treasures were hidden in three grains of salt,
an eye like a rusted keyhole to gaze at the most beautiful
    future
and a buried mirror where the word of supreme power
    was written.
You invented games, temptations, forms of disobedience.
So many years were shared in parties and goodbyes
the song shattered into fragments when your hand
    slipped out of mine.
Sisters of wind gusts and shivering, my sisters,
I hear them singing from the thick scrub of my
    abandoned night.
I know they come back now to refute my loneliness,
to fulfil the pact our blood sealed till after the world,
till we complete the song anew.

MAROSA DI GIORGIO

FUNERAL CARRIAGES LADEN WITH WATERMELONS

At midday, jagged magnolias and pears, topazes with feet and with wings; lilies, bright, red, half-open; the same old house, the familiar patio, looked like paradise, with the shining of its branches, clusters of grapes, stars among the leaves, their five-pointed forms mirrored on the floors.

And the baby with its feathers. No one knew if it was a boy or a girl. The baby among the creams. White, light blue, pink. If it was a woman or a man. The baby in its lace veils, its yolks and whites, its "bridal garlands".

Longing was, there, served up.

That was it, precisely.

They rang the alarm bells. When the murder, the rape of the baby; the devouring, the consumption. Alarm bells rang out, when it was the visitation for the baby, and everything else.

The fruit vanished. The house was grey, tiny. Just like before, more than before.

A minute went by.

I don't know if a day, if years went by.

And God forgave. You could hear the rustle of his wings descending along the grapes.

God burnt the sin,

wiped it out,

burnt it,

left it white, like snow, like foam.

* * *

Bats flew by, caught in the clothes of cows, gazelles; I freed some when I could.

And others, more domesticated, hung head-down in the kitchen; papa gave them wine and cigarettes. Us women, more naïve, laid out roses and wallflowers so the intense perfume of blood and sugar of those flowers, might calm them.

One day one bit me; but I remained unharmed. I've heard, yes, that "the children of night make their own music". But I don't participate in the banquet. I am here as a witness. Or I participate, and don't know it.

* * *

What a strange species is the species angel. When I was born I heard them say "Angel", "Angels", or other names. "Spikenard", "Iris". Foam that grows on branches, most delicate porcelain increasing all by itself. Spikenard. Iris.

And in the dogs' eyes, too, there are angels.

Oh they were tall, wearing feathers and gauze, long long wings, grey eyes. They went with us to school (each of us had one), to the girls' dance, to my successive parallel weddings, I counted them already one by one.

Where the bridegrooms were lizards, eucalypts or carnations.

And to the great wedding with the Cat Montes; my mother was frightened and took my hand, and papa didn't dare go.

They flew all around nearby. The entrance to the grove, the kitchen, the oven with small skulls inside, with captured doves.

They were present at the ceremony and the rites.

And with their silent power they saved me.

* * *

A flower appeared in the water. A burning, dazzling rose. Round or oval, from one moment to another. With no roots, there on a black leaf. A boy discovered it and screamed that something strange was in the water, and his mother gave him a gentle smack, saying it was just a flower. Later, she realized it had the look of sorcery.

I stripped off my clothes and swam, I who don't know how to swim; I flew, I who could never fly. But between the flower and me there was always a distance; however much my fingers stretched out they could never reach it.

A large part of the day sped by; there was now a disturbance in the village.

And the flower rose up, almost brushing our eyes, it rose with all its crests in flame. The children, then, thought it was a kite. The grown ups, then, thought it was a kite.

Higher up, it resembled the moon, and higher still, a star, and then it slipped into nothingness.

Years pass. We go on exploring minutely, uselessly, the lake, the air, the nothingness.

* * *

The thief was golden. He was a pink thief.

It seems he reached the house in the afternoon. With all his evil deeds, prewritten already. And he rolled himself up in a hole in the wall, into a spiral, a snail.

Only his eyes stuck out like two black buttons. So I saw him clearly. But I thought it was something strange that had begun to form there, an animal never seen before. And I said nothing.

As night sunk, when wind was rocking the trees and pears and roses fell, he came out of his hiding place, and brandished a knife. His back was golden. He wore a pink-coloured shawl. He took a few steps, and from the cupboard eggs and plates fell, and out of the wardrobe bats and chicks flew.

Papa stood up, wobbling on his feet; mama screamed; my grandparents muttered something in their sleep; the other girls screamed and fell asleep, screamed and fell asleep. I, said nothing.

By midnight, he'd now triumphed over everyone. And went away, with his sharp blades, with his shawl.

* * *

What a strange night it was when grandfather died. Drops, white stones, fell from the lemon trees and the rosebush. Rats came out of the cupboard; a dozen small cups, the tiny glasses, always twelve; liquors of all colours turned black.

Aunt Joseph let out a scream beside the corpse. Us girls were screaming too. Unexpectedly the most distant aunts turned up, cousins of cousins, suddenly, in one minute, as if they'd been travelling on horseback or on butterflies. And neighbours from the most distant farms, and even from farms under the earth, came in their funeral carriages, laden with watermelons.

I saw someone, the strangest person, inside the mirror; I focussed carefully to see if it was a reflection; but there was no one there like him.

But then, at dawn, the strangers left. All of them. And we lay down. Each of us in her own bed. And we slept, for a few hours, very deeply.

And there between us lay grandfather, dead.

* * *

I stood motionless, with my long red curls, in the gardens of uncle Juan; next to me, bloodroots and everlastings, also reddish.

Those who went past me thought I was a doll, a painting, an angel, one of the many angels always to be found in rosebushes and nests. And they looked at me with a certain seriousness and devotion. And all around there were nesting boxes with eggs of varying size, all extremely delicate. I saw miraculous things flickering.

And I wanted to move, to go away; but no one called me, because no one believed in me,

. . . no one calls me,

night is about to fall.

And I remain motionless.

Inside my white dress, inside my red hat.

* * *

Through the immeasurable forest. I saw its end and couldn't reach it. With a small basket of red strawberries. And butterflies, souls, of all colours; some were landing on me.

The train, that monster, split the forest as if it was about to kill it, (there were now two forests), and vanished into infinity.

Again, an immense silence.

The tallest trees reached the sky, reached the houses of the saints.

And fleeing school, fleeing mama, I wandered about in my short red dress, with my little basket of black mulberries.

And from the thickest part of the woods stepped the Wolf, his pointy face, sunken eyes; but I didn't turn back or stop looking.

And every day, the same comedy, the same ritual.

Rosa and the wolf.

Half and half.

* * *

When I was six or eight years old, grandmother ordered a hare suit so I could be free from all evil. And so she made a sack of hare skin and adjusted it, and inside she placed pencils and books.

At dawn, before dawn, during the night, dressed like that, I left for school, moving on all fours, through the glistening grass-blades and the dahlias. Hundreds of metres; sometimes I stopped and prepared coffee in a small flask, and went on.

But, one time, the wild boys discovered me.

They screamed out: Look, it's Rosa the hare; it's the hare, the hare; it's the hare! And they surrounded me.

The stars stretched out their branches, so I could climb on board and escape with them.

But dawn had begun painting its colours.

And you could see the sacrifice in the scrub.

* * *

We went on a visit. Mama in high heels over the rough stones, through the tall grass. Mama with feathers in her hat. And Nidia and I, in front, dressed in the same fashion. Far off, black eucalypts, clumps of broom, Presences.

When we reached the house we'd visit, they peered out to see who we were.

And with great courtesy they led us to the dining room. Nidia and I wore a white organdie bow over our forehead. And in the paintings, always the same thing: a bleeding duck, a melon, a bunch of grapes. And in the small baskets, also, bunches of grapes.

The conversation, an hour and a half, was about strange, suitably appropriate, things.

Then the liquor cabinet with its tiny glasses, and the pastries which we barely touched, glancing at mama from the corner of our eyes; and blushing like cherries. And the farewells all the way to the front gate. Mama walked, laboriously, through the tall grass. Nidia and I in front, almost identical. Nidia a little smaller. And, amazed, we saw stains of colour in the sky, the scrub so dark, and finally a weasel who raced past, her eyes closed, like a madwoman, a chicken in her mouth.

* * *

A mysterious longing came over me to see fruit, to eat fruit; I left the house and made for the forest. I caught an apple, a quince, a cherry with its blue hood. I roasted a dahlia, lightly, and ate it; I drank a rose in one gulp; I saw peaches and their ochre wine, grapes, red, black, white; figs that provide equal shelter to the Devil and Saint John, and bunches of bananas and loquats; dates fell into my blouse.

Wings of astonishing whiteness grew out of me, my dress grew. I started to fly. I didn't want to come back, ever. I landed on a roof; they thought I was a stork, a tall angel; the women screamed; the men circled with dark plans.

I couldn't return now.

I go on, I go on.

People are up late, coming back from parties;
and I return overhead, flying.

* * *

I want to enter a garden of dark roses, round, oval, red, velvet, like those I saw as a small child, with the fragrance of wine, of grapes and apple, that, I don't know why, they used to call Stars. Of France. To sit there, with no one seeing me. And they would go past, so close, almost brushing me, saying, "Come out!", "Come out!" and then calling, "She must be hiding!", "She must be asleep!"

And smoke comes from the house, a smell of rice and spikenard, of puddings, a counterpoint of owls and violins.

And, at midnight, to appear with an extraordinary smile, in the midst of weeping, lavender, white pastry, and say: You were looking at me and didn't see me.

* * *

He came galloping with a dead lamb. Down the valley, down the lanes between the fields. With the dead child whose head wobbled back and forth.

There were so many stars and blue flowers of the mio-mio; in the paddocks, so many flowers and the tiniest insects.

Many sinned in the fields, others fished in the fields, they set out hooks and hunted rats, small hares which they brought back to their houses, half dead, half alive.

Everyone wanted to copulate, to eat, to kill.

But it was like a dream that starts and vanishes.

* * *

It was a morning with some rain, and wind. The spurge showed its black fruit and hard leaves, a type of punishment. It looked like a juniper bush about to offer some black diabolic drink.

As if in a nightmare the little white hen walked towards it; I called it, but it didn't turn its small head where madness had already built its nest; I saw its delicate legs, its light dress.

I wanted to go. And immediately large spider webs appeared, filled with pearls and gems, stiff and very beautiful. In whatever direction I wanted to leave there was one of these webs. Someone constructed them out of their imagination, to stop me going.

And in the spurge, in the juniper, the white dove was no more.

* * *

The bride of the orchards was tall, slender, very beautiful; her hair gathered at her neck in a type of bun; she wore a black dress, a white shawl. She had been born in that house; she knew how to cook, knit, sew, look after the brooms, she didn't know how to write, she knew how to pray.

(The bridegroom came from only a few metres away.)

To enter the church she had to bend down, well, the door was tiny and she was very tall. She wore a black dress, a white shawl. And for a bouquet, the florets of a cauliflower: long grey leaves, pinkish white, curled over, mother-of-pearl; on them grains of rice fell, and farewells and tears.

* * *

The wasps were extremely delicate. Like angels, many fitted on the head of a pin. All of them resembled young ladies, dancing teachers. I imitated their murmuring rather well. They circled the apple's white flowers, the quince's ochre flowers, the pomegranate's hard red roses. Or in the tiny fountains where my cousins, my sisters and I gazed at them, our hands on our chins. Compared to them we were giants, monsters. But the most wondrous thing was the cartons they made; almost in one stroke, their palaces of thick grey paper appeared, among the leaves, and, inside them, plates of honey.

Meanwhile, the lizard continued hunting for hen's eggs, warm tid-bits; snakes blue as fire crossed the path, curly, delicately crafted carnations, looking like bowls of fruit and rice, shot up.

The world, all of it, welcoming, magical.

And one face, separated, the only one painted, walked among the leaves, eyes downcast, red mouth open.

And when it had already gone by
it walked past one more time.

* * *

At night, bats arrived.

Even if I don't call them, they, just the same, come.

They came with black wings and bunches of grapes.

They fell inside my white dress. Among all the roses and camellias I gathered during those years. And into the basket of carnations and freesias. The Virgin Mary screamed and fled through all the rooms, her hair down, brushing the floor and the dahlias.

The pearls, almonds and pastries, glass fruit and syrup that lived in fruit bowls and porcelain jars, all turned black, then clear once more, but somehow dead.

I stood up. My white handkerchief and my throat were dripping blood.

* * *

Of all the cousins who came to visit my mother when we lived in the country, one remains engraved in my mind.

Always, she'd arrive with a group; it was obvious she didn't dare cross the fields on her own. She used to wear brown dresses, with a streaked pattern, two aprons in the same colours, a cap like a pilot's, glasses, and instead of a nose she had a beak, hard, red, orange-coloured. A boy secretly drew a picture of her, but tore it up because he was frightened.

Otherwise, she was sweet, she smiled. She brought basil as a present, and mint. And small packets of sweets and amethysts.

* * *

We decide to continue stealing. But separately. Estrella on her own; and I by myself. Some nights are propitious. The sky orange-coloured, pink cyclamen. The oranges, absolutely black. The birds return; you have to be careful because of their whistling, their spinning around. I know which branch I'll choose. I don't know where Estrella will go. The owners of the orchards walk by. With their shoulder bags and trays. They are carrying a new-born lamb or one that's just been sacrificed. Pears and apples, bunches of lilacs. Is there going to be a wedding? At midnight everything is completely still. I climb down. I find a small path and look to see if, at the next moment, Estrella will come. I brush past the broad leaves of the spurge and the violets' round leaves. I enter the house; no time to hesitate. Lightly I continue above cupboards and wardrobes, I steal what is in the boxes. Someone lets out a shriek; others cry out. I flee. I don't know if they are there with axes or if it was only a cry.

The moon leaves everything white, and the hiding places, blacker.

Estrella goes by, quickly, with her load.
And we disappear into the ground.

* * *

When I was an owl I observed everything with my hot
and cold pupil; no being, no thing was lost on me. I floated
ahead of anyone walking by in the fields, my double cape
open, my white legs half open; like a woman. And before I
let out the petrifying scream, all fled to the gold mountain,
to the mountain of shadows, saying: And that thing in
mid-air like a star?

But also, I was a girl there in the house.

Mama kept the mystery to herself.

And looked at God, weeping.

* * *

They appeared, suddenly, like all the things in my
life. Black, white, with silken shawls. In the middle of the
field, the lake in the field, the house. Water birds gazing
downwards, thoughtfully. Above tall claws. They looked
like willows, men, the most different things. We could
see them through the windows and in the bedrooms the
gossip went on. What did they predict? Rain? Wind? The
coming summer, the winter beyond that?

One day, one came by himself, a black one. And violent
people killed him. A girl saw the murder from far away.
(Myself). And doesn't forget.

My life comes and goes.

Comes, goes.

And, always, there is a black bird that falls. And falls.

* * *

I opened my wings, next to the roof, and hit myself. Brown with stains of cherries and unknown numbers.

The mother of the family and the children (who already went to school) saw they were unknown numbers.

They wanted to tear my wings off.

I don't exactly know what they said.

I was there, above them, weightless.

The wind came in.

The father of the family came in.

They brought in some gadgets; I don't exactly know what they said.

He looked at me. Maybe he fell into a space of enchantment and grief. To him I looked like a woman in a ballroom dress.

The light went out.

What had they decided?

In the darkness I turned black, and became much larger; and the edges of my wings gave off light. I couldn't leave because Things Done had placed me there.

They were not going to bed.

I remained black, motionless and changing.

* * *

Under their leaves the pumpkin were flat, like plates.

Their backs, round, orange-coloured, their chests, round, orange-coloured; they looked like the shield of Achilles, shining in the sun. Butterflies and roses came. Cows with evil plans. Hares in dark-brown glasses. My grandmother, Señora Rosa, arrived and paid no attention to any of this. She put some of them in the bottom of her baskets. She brought them home, divided them, transformed them into honey and fairies. She invited me.

I was touched. I almost went in, bewitched, as you see me.

* * *

The war's begun, again, she said stepping out from the magnolias into the living room, into the black kitchen where so many things were transformed. One made off with a bunch of grapes; another, with I don't know what; another with a hen and its egg. In the dazzling black air, once more, everything began. But I, what have I done?, I said.

And the sound of distant guns was heard. I was naked, as always, wearing only the coral necklace, a delicate doll on the altar. Yet, through the window which had been left open, the rix appeared, its braids around its forehead, and also naked; so I stepped into the garden; there was a great tumult. Wine flowed everywhere. With its rose fragrance. Its strawberry fragrance. Its soul fragrance. I flew overhead like a dragonfly, dressed in jewels from the sea, little animals, pink, exquisite. A great silence; and occasionally, from the trees an explosion of stars erupted. Till, finally, it ended. The king went away, turned his back on us. Many corpses were left against the door and, among them, plants had already started being born.

One person went off with I don't know what.

Another, with a goose.

Another, with shears to cut the honeysuckle and the old festive mistletoe.

I returned to the living room, the kitchen; in the shining black air everything was beginning once more.

* * *

A frightening black butterfly arrived during the night and perched on the roof. It knew all the sexual games. Terrified, we acted stupid. But it came down; till it murmured something; one person, it hit in the face; it landed on another's chest; I ran, calling out for someone who wasn't there, just the empty house, the wind.

It approached me, threatened me; each one of us, it approached and threatened. It was active all through the night; step by step, it carried out its plans. At dawn it vanished over the treetops.

We bolted the windows and the blinds twice. That day might never come again. We fled to the darkness, crazy with fear and shame.

* * *

Papa, I'm feverish, all hot and cold; take care of the house, the little animals, the mice (black, white, brownish, grey), leave them food, bread, syrup, confetti.

. . . But you go on digging up the earth in the orange garden.

I watch you through the enormous window.

You go on and on in the impressive orange garden.

You don't come to see if I'm asleep, if I'm getting better, getting married, am dying, have fallen out of bed.

Days, months, years pass by.

Kites hang from the roof, delicate and blue, with chiffon tails, golden eyes.

There are jasmines on the altar. (A small basket). Mama is saying very strange things about them.

And you say nothing,

aren't you coming to listen?

* * *

It will seem a lie. But we come from a time where the Weasel and Maria Perla could be.

As the sun sets they appear in the lanes. At opposite ends of the lane, though they seem to be walking together. Their face so tight-pinched, drops of honey on the snout, a bob of red hair round their ears.

Where are they going? To rosary? To the abattoir?

Will they steal our sweet bread, the tiny roses that opened just a minute ago?

The village chatters away below the moon.

And its ancient inhabitants – the most ancient inhabitants – continue on unexpectedly.

* * *

Along the wire fences, glittering sinister spiderwebs. These weavers respond to the world with their silverwork. And Luck places gems and pearls with absolute certainty; only where they should go.

Along the wire fences are the remains of weasels and hummingbirds (which have come to rest here, in their nocturnal flights).

And a cloud drifts down, calm and hard-working, like a woman, a real person; it steals some things, some remnants. It leaves others. Snails (they disappear quickly, into the field). And a diminutive angel that we bring home and give a name to, Lilam. It is like a delicate doll, with tiny gold wings and hair the same. It's there, motionless, for hours, above the furniture. Or it flies on the breeze through the rooms, before our dazzled gaze.

* * *

During the night I heard a noise. I knew something had changed in the garden. I went there, in the greatest darkness. I waited trembling. At dawn I saw what it was. A butterfly was being born. I wanted to protect it, to bring it inside, before the degenerate men who are always about could appear. But who embraces a butterfly, who carries a soul in their hands? Then, I noticed its wings stretching upwards, growing visibly, black, purple; turning into sacred pink diamonds. Now other people had stopped, just nearby, motionless with horror. On its wings it had snow-coloured stripes, with confused stories, written or painted, that everyone was trying to decipher. And the wings rose between the trees, I don't know how, sprinkled with precious stones; the wings reached the sun; and in the following hours, days or months, since we'd lost the idea of time, there was always a kind of mist, a soft darkness. I tried to go, I took my things and left the garden. But along the road they stopped me, telling me I must go back, since I was the one who'd discovered this.

And so, by night, I hear murmuring, buzzing, and at dawn I see wings rise, black, purple, pink, golden, with stories of saints inscribed against the light.

THE MOTH

To visit those uncles we always had to go at night; we'd travel in the moonlight as far as the black orange tree, as the mushrooms that rose open and tall with the light grace of a lily.

The kitchen, empty at that hour. Likewise the sanctuary and shed. In the bedroom the uncles were sleeping soundly; without waking, out of their deepest sleep they'd say:

– Hello! Have you come? Why don't you come more often?

– . . .

– Is that you here? Eat something.

– We're already eating.

– There's rice and milk on the table.

– We've seen it.

– Goodbye then. Come back soon.

– Goodbye, goodbye.

We returned to the black orange tree and the flowering mushrooms, walking very quickly, before the moon could go down into the mountain cave and we'd be stranded with no direction.

* * *

Someone stepped into the dark bedroom, without opening the door, and began combing my hair. I, strangely, did almost nothing to defend myself.

Strand by strand he combed my hair, all the way to the tip, even the bangs, the curls, ringlets, and once more all the way down. The comb was opaque, sometimes glittering like coral.

I did almost nothing to free myself, till the hair was straight and fully stretched out, and it touched the floor and flowed on like a river.

And whoever combed me vanished in the dark – without opening the door – just as they had come.

* * *

The sombre woodcutter loomed up in the late afternoon.

She had just sat down near the door.

He was black from the mountain sun. He climbed down from his cart and said:

– Do you want wood? She: No, no. I'm alone. Papa isn't here.

He put his reptile hand on the door and it gave way, and salad could be seen, already made, on the table.

The salad was green like fire and red like sin.

The salad was red like fire and green like sin.

She offered him some to dispel other thoughts.

He said: No, no, I don't want anything.

And he lifted her up in the air like a doll.

In her tiny trembling voice she called out: – This is the hour when papa comes home!

But he didn't hear a word.

Outside, the wind rocked the cane field and the small ponds where till only a moment ago she had been playing.

* * *

The groves of rubber trees, eggplants, violets and grapes are amazing.

Star animals have fallen into the nets and can't escape.

The saints, in the air, look on with their light-blue eyes, impassive. And opposite, the women saints form a different line, their wings lowered, and their hair flowing down their wings.

* * *

Diamena came in with the bones. It was in the tiny house in the deepest part of the Apuan night. Diamena set the plate down on the table. They were all there. The parents: Domenico and Maria; the sons: Pascual, Pedro, Enrique, Ernesto, Albino, Hector; the daughters: Divina, Rosa, Iride.

Diamena set down the plate with the bones.

Outside, a fleeting animal, a white blur, was moving around; its dazzling coat reached the ground; or it was dark and small, and came in through the window and went for the plate. Diamena took the plate away.

Mother and the girls called out: Diamena, go outside; the wind's coming in!

Diamena took the plate and went out.

It was in the deepest part of the Apuan night, and things like that happened.

* * *

For some time they had been waiting for the Soul. And the Soul never came. Mama made coloured lollies and kept them in black boxes, and on a plate she laid out candles of different sizes and shapes. And what would the soul be like? Would its feet be gold and silver? Would it wear fine crystal crowns? Be woven in white thread like some kind of lace? With jasmine instead of bones?

To await its arrival they planted rosebushes right across the meadow and a sea of gladioli. There was a ship among the grass, and rats ruled the sea (the short-lived pink sea of the orchards).

But the Soul refused to appear.

Until one afternoon there it was, seated suddenly in our midst!

The stars fell, every which way, like peas and corn; the ship of the fields had sailed right up to the window and its sails darkened everything; the gladioli tried to save themselves and fled south; but halfway through their journey they died, frozen already, with a sound like paper crumbling.

Each one of the house's inhabitants began screaming; but not all together, (and this is the strange thing), just one by one.

I was the last to scream and, without wanting to, I touched one of the Soul's hands: the hand had many many fingers, a multitude, like pistols, countless.

And the Soul looked at me and left.

* * *

It was not often a soul came to visit. Some people waited years for one all in vain. And, without wanting to, I met one. It rose up out of a melon, like a thread of silk, like fine lace. I leapt over the leaves, the other melons, into red amber liquid; I saw a pumpkin, about a metre high, narrow, a heavy dark green, almost black, it looked like a small piece of furniture, a closet, to hide the most secret of things: I bumped into it and it gave no response. But I was scrambling to get away, I passed the meadow and its red daisies; I saw the water partridges swimming with their shoes on; they were coming and going continuously, as if they'd lost all sense; they always did that.

I was almost home, but I was afraid to go inside and fled; I ran to the forest, to my favourite tree, climbed it, curled up tight.

But it was terrible, oh, hours and hours went by and night was about to fall. I heard a whistling in the grass, something was climbing the tree, an insect with pearls, that wasn't an insect, there above my temples.

* * *

I met the soul halfway through eating my soup, while sticking a fork into a piece of meat, into a potato.

The others at the table were talking about the day's events. It had been an overcast day. Planting potatoes, spring onions. In the large garden, gladioli. And again, spring onions.

It was a conversation among farmers.

And the hundred-year-old cupboards with blonde-coloured honey inside, blonder than honey, and the decanter, a deep grape-blue.

And in the soup I saw some type of building that was alive, growing bigger and then it opened, a strip of cloth that, as it unrolled, would never reach an end. I pressed and poked it, subdued it.

I hid what I was doing, pretended to be eating, drinking, gazing outside.

The others at the table said: Eat, Little Rosa. Eat your soup, rosy rosary, our star.

And I, hiding it all as best I could.

* * *

The most tremendous thing, of course, was the apparition of God; in the most intimate room, the final resting place, God appeared with the precious stones.

It was one evening. The women who were visiting had gone, and the lilies were lifting their pale bells into the air, and she stopped motionless, in the garden.

From there, the lambs, realising what was happening,

came in a committee, or one by one; they gazed at her as if they had never seen her before, their narrow eyes wide open behind their wool.

* * *

When I was born there were lots and lots of figs. That can't be, they'd tell me, it was winter and cold.

Nevertheless that's how it was; they were on all the trees, even those that weren't fig trees, and inside flowers. Dark, light blue or pink: some from their beginning had a violet or a fly stuck to them. Or, at their centre, they secreted a pearl (the pearl never came out completely). Or they'd break loose and spin like stars wrapped in rings of colour, till, almost lifeless, they'd go back into their place.

You could smell a fragrance of fine liquor and lilies.

Crying for the first time, it was a few minutes after my birth, I said to my mother: There's figs.

And my mother smiled at my grandmother Rosa, and said: Look at what she's said.

And my grandmother came close, too close, her eyes lowered, her smile fixed, wearing a tremendous crown of black figs, thick and tormented.

* * *

During the night, at dawn, they brought clothes, costumes; they made them with percale, with "radiant"; pink percale, pale green; "radiant" that was always black as roses. They left them on the floor, on the ground, on the table and sofa.

At dawn I cried out: Mama, Nidia! Come quick! There's costumes!

And each one of us cherished the secret hope of wearing one or several of them over the following days and years.

But these clothes could not be worn.

They were like creatures of unreality, creatures of tragedy.

* * *

When one of us died, everything turned black. The other owners of small farms came and sat in a circle, and every half hour coffee was served in glasses, that, years later, when we gave up the farmhouse, were still hanging on the walls. The wind from some crack made an unusual sound; and further off, the laurels and the grasses rocked.

And we were all silent.

And before dawn when the first faint light began to appear, some small, very stylish birds soared upwards. At first we took them for hummingbirds, and then they turned out to be parrots, fine and frail and very beautiful; sparkling like precious stones they flew and flew above the one lying there under his black coverlet (many thought they were dreaming this), but I saw it was true, and when the birds left, I left too, and followed them for a little into the gardens and saw they were carrying the soul (this was like a spider web): all of them were helping carry it, maybe to some far off hiding place.

*　*　*

On the day of the martyrdom black dust went up into the sky, and then, white dust went up into the sky.

And at that moment the victim was bound, and the relatives fled towards the geranium beds, but couldn't make their way into them; they were frozen in their frantic rush to escape.

And it took nearly half an hour to cut off the head, since, there were various difficulties, till it fell into a basket, and the massive quavering body was lifted up. And others (greedily) carried off buckets of blood.

But, inside the house, in a corner, someone burst into tears, their mouth twisted, weeping on and on; and they didn't want to touch any meals after that.

And years later, they said they could still hear the screams of the victim, and above all, one of the screams.

*　*　*

At sunset, walking near the house, she saw a butterfly had settled on her skirt, when she looked again there were now two; she wanted to shake out her pinafore, and now there were two more; these butterflies were black with yellow markings, and they kept appearing two by two, suddenly there, motionless, paralysed.

Again she looked closely and now they covered all her dress, her hair and forehead.

When she raised her eyes she saw the butterflies – all black and yellow – forming a chlamys, a pyramid. If one was light blue or pink (something she noticed), the others, through some influence whose working was unknown, made them disappear, dissolved them.

So matters stood, grandfather appeared; when he saw this he began to talk, very rapidly, in another language, and vanished from sight. Grandmother entered, made a heartrending gesture, backing away. Auntie (Josefa) came; she was a dreamer and began to say: How beautiful they are!

But, her face froze and she vanished into the wind.

Her sister and cousin appeared; just barely young girls; and when they saw everything, they stretched out their hands towards these ladies with wings and antennae, cautiously like someone about to pick roses from a rosebush, frightened by the thorns. But then, they drew back, and without turning round fled. They cried out: Goodbye! . . . In a voice that seemed to be travelling through different layers of cloud and dust.

At sunset. Alone with her fate.

* * *

The lady poets with their long long hair, grey with the odd black thread, and jasmine covering their faces, sitting on the threshold of the oldest house.

A fine rain fell like dust on the dark plants, and from the sky rice fell, which they boiled in a pot.

Now the final sheaf of pages had been started.

An enormous butterfly, very white and fragile, rose suddenly out of them; or, the opposite, they had come out of it.

This butterfly encompassed all the wind, the infinite, and so, distressed, it flew away, deep into itself.

* * *

Walking through the woods at sunset we met various Virgins – though there was only one – sitting or kneeling, here and there; nearly always kneeling.

They were thin and very young, and the colour of their skin and clothes, grey pink, mother-of-pearl, pink iris. In the laps of their dresses they always had an egg, a carnation, an amethyst.

Mama screamed: "It's the Virgin! It's the Virgin!"

And these words The Virgin sunk into my forehead, like a stone, like a star.

And under bright and darkening clouds, we ran home, a sliver of fear within us, the Virgins by our side.

* * *

The soul of Clementina Médici is a grey, white chiffon, that comes in metres and metres, sometimes, fringed with coloured threads; sometimes, with an olive tree from Jerusalem. In a knot in this silk the Devil nests; I'm bewildered by his unveilings, his shimmerings. I'd like to flee, but Clementina Médici My Mother, dresses me as a bride, head to foot, at each moment; I'm wearing something white in front of my eyes; I'd like to run away, but it's impossible; I walk in this veil, I perish, revive, vanish, like a tiny butterfly in a garden.

* * *

When she was born the wolf appeared. It was a Sunday at midday – eleven thirty, brilliant light – and her mother saw through the windowpane, the pointed snout, and in its fur, spikes of frost, and screamed; but, they gave her a potion that put her pleasantly to sleep.

The wolf was there at her baptism and communion; baptism, in her long baby's dress; first communion, with her pink dress. No one saw the wolf; only his pointy ears stuck out from under things.

He followed her to school, hiding behind rosebushes and cabbages; he spied on her during parties after exams, when she trembled a little.

He spotted her first boyfriend, and the second one, and the third, who only gazed at her through the front gate. She in the elusive organdie wrapping that they wore back then, girls in gardens. And pearls, on her head, in her décolletage, the hem of her dress, heavy dazzling pearls (they were the one thing that held her dress up). When she moved she would lose one or other of the pearls. But the boyfriends disappeared; no one knew why.

Her friends got married; one after the other; she went to the lavish parties; she was present at the birth of each one of their children.

And the years went by, flew by, and she too in her strangeness. One day she turned around and said to someone: It's the wolf.

Though in truth she had never seen a wolf.

Until an extraordinary night came, with camellias and stars. An extraordinary night came.

Behind the front gate the wolf appeared; suddenly he was there like a boyfriend, like a man he spoke in a soft convincing voice. He said: Come. She obeyed; a pearl fell off. It was gone. He said: Here?

But, they walked past camellias and rosebushes, completely black in the darkness, till they reached a hollow that seemed dug especially. She knelt down; he knelt down. He pulled out his long tongue and licked her. He said to her: How do you want this?

She made no reply. She was a queen. Only the gentle smile she had seen on her friends' faces at their weddings.

He tore off one hand, and the other hand; one foot, the other foot. He looked at her like that for a moment. Then he tore off her head; her eyes (he placed one to each side); he tore out her ribs and everything.

But, most of all, he devoured her blood, rapidly, with sure skill and the utmost virility.

Her hair was a long braid of garlic. Her face square, but sometimes oval. She appeared beside the jasmine, the flowers of Cambray, that rose from the black leaves, like wrinkled organdie.

As she was never married or had a boyfriend they called her the Virgin of the Farms. And everyone loved her and hated her at the same time, without her noticing this.

Still, they built a church, a small one, so she would have somewhere to eat and sleep; she ate candles, squares of crêpe, and some light-blue or white jasmine.

But, life on the farms changed.

The citadel moved forward towards where the gardens were, and where before there had been basil there was pink marble.

Yet, she remained motionless.

On her shoulder the long braid of garlic, and on the hems of her dress, jasmine, fresh herbs, dried herbs, and unhatched eggs.

A butterfly I had seen many many years ago appeared; but, now, in a photograph. Who had taken it and how did it come to be there?

The butterfly came out of the postage stamp; and flew round and round, it performed the pantomime of its life, becoming once more only an image.

The kings were making their sumptuous return to their homes. And I, on the edge of my bed, analysed all the events of that morning.

* * *

They were weaving God with a strong black thread that also turned blue; others fished for him with a golden thread, filigreed; others with squares of organdie that resembled a cloud.

And some people wove him using little skeins of thread of all colours. And it was these who created a more blazing divinity.

* * *

She drank tea, she went to school. But, suddenly, her wing began to shine. (Her mother was distraught.) It appeared in a corner of the home, inside or outside, or in both places, at the same time; it wasn't clear.

Inside her guts (they could be seen through the flimsy organdie veil of her dress) and without anyone having touched her, she gave birth to creatures and things, cows, dolls, and other blue or multicoloured virgins; she screamed as she gave birth to them, and immediately she was a different length.

And once again she drank tea, went to school.

But for a short time.

*   *   *

A long tradition of dahlias, "feathers", roses, mushrooms higher than the windows. A column of smoke rises from inside the earth, signalling a village there.

It's the afternoon of honeysuckle and cats. It's the afternoon.

Black calf with white mask, with pale mask, tied up facing the door.

I remember you.

What I most remember is the twisted fingers of the dahlias.

And the drumming of your steps going nowhere.

*   *   *

The devil was dancing on lemons of blue fire, he was dancing in the perfume, on the dead leaves, on the freesias.

I hid by the wall, astonished at the gigantic bird, the man with hoof and wings, whose unknown face was like my father's, like that of my friends and my enemies.

Each time I made myself smaller and smaller. He was dancing and, while dancing, caught dahlias, roses, and gulped them down as if they were souls.

Till he stretched back and fell asleep, looking like a handsome young squire, all mint and flower-buds.

Then I got up, I too began dancing.

But, as if nothing had happened, all was as still as ever.

The doves' eggs fine as sugar. And the carnation made of air.

When we were more or less little kids, or more or less grown-ups, in a confused zone, we wanted to catch the moon. We piled up cones and square blocks, and more cones and square blocks, that then fell down, and cardboard steps that fell down and other schemes. Till Miguel got the idea of shooting it down with a rifle (found inside a horse's skeleton), and then it would come down like a pomegranate loosing its seeds, but that didn't work either. Even worse, one of our distant neighbours came over, and told us off very sternly; we answered with some gibberish or other.

Then, I remembered a very frightening black thread, with which mother performed certain tasks, and, spiriting it away, we made shirts and wings that we armed with small sticks, and making the most of a favourable gust, with a big push, we were able to climb higher and higher, till we reached the black, silvery night. And we began circling the moon, beating our wings against it over and over; it was smooth as a mirror and rough as a loaf of bread; it gave off an emerald-like, tourmaline-like darkness, a cold pink light, and there was no way to conquer it, till Miguel grabbed hold of it and detached it; you mustn't forget it was hanging only from the air.

And so the descent began, lower and lower all the time, we were frightened Miguel would run off, would never say that we'd all reached the moon together.

* * *

Ah, with so many trees of the same family, only on one did the red fruit appear. And that only once in a while, once in many years; when its green hood opened, it could be seen shining like a live coal or a rose.

And so we were all frightened, as if the end of the world was about to happen, as if it was a comet with a fateful tail.

Yet only small everyday things happened; nothing good or bad happened. Till on the morning of some day or other, that fruit was no longer seen.

* * *

The carnation appeared one morning flying; maybe it came from very far away; its wings short and round; bright red like a man, a woman's pale pink. You couldn't see if it travelled alone, or with a passenger; if it had a mission, or was flying just to fly.

The house owners held out their frying pans, to see if it would fall and cook itself, turning into second lunch or desert. The first Communion girls half opened their lips as if it was the host. It hit me on the forehead; its oily fragrance, its crackling sound like embers, penetrated my throat; I opened my fingers; it split in half; I had one piece in each hand, but it joined back together and flew off.

All the neighbours came out of their houses, walked to the open field. With glasses. To watch the flight of the carnation.

* * *

With the tallest of trees, Pruzzo's farm was so beautiful! My grandmother and I would sneak in cautiously like thieves. There, the hummingbirds were red, bright vermillion. There were blue-green ones and gold ones, but most were red. They crossed the air like arrows, meddling with the roses and narcissi.

From the darkness Alsatians peered out with eyes that shone like jewels.

In the air, tiny glistening birds. And us on another's land, in suspense, motionless, trembling slightly.

* * *

Mother-of-pearl: pink, pale dark-green, grey. Empty clams all over the farm, the sombre breakwater and moonlight. Were they the Virgin's nest?

Also the dead people of the house: grandfathers, uncles, cousins, were turning into mother-of-pearl. They floated there by the black figs and the broom. But, however much I stretched out my arm towards That, I never reached it, even using a ladder, even using a tower.

* * *

In the centre the lake, motionless as a mirror.

Round it, mangled, tangled webs from which peppers burst and blazed; green ones, bright red ones, the dazzling sheen of roses and tomatoes. Each one was burning, was a live ember: had a mouth, little teeth, a titillating tongue.

And the butterfly singers, singing butterflies – whoever listens to them is condemned – and I listened to many. I wore hats on my head.

From the distance, across the infinite tangle of vines, I could hear my relatives; they said: Be careful. You've gone out without sandals or bonnet. Be careful.

And I could hear them there, next to me. As if the vines were telephones.

Frightened I steadied my almond-like foot; my hand too. And I answered on the telephone of the vines, lying I answered them: There's nothing to be careful about. Nothing's there. Nothing brushed me. All I saw was roses. And then softly, darkly I said: I'm lying.

* * *

The "mulita" armadillo turned a very beautiful pale green, almost light blue, in the paroxysm of fear. With its tiny hands it ran down the paths, through the rosebushes; and hid, and reappeared, transformed now to gold, to precious stones, to a small box with links and studs.

And once more it scurried further down and reappeared, its small, brown, everyday plates rattling in the cold night.

And again it went further down towards the place of the roots, where poisonous mushrooms and pink-coloured mushrooms are born.

But hunting dogs were leaping off the terraces; and men with lamps and sticks leapt out of the trees.

. . . Its body was served with violets on china plates, alongside wine and gentle conversations. For the twenty minutes of the meal.

* * *

So strange the bovine cry, the bellowing of cows at nightfall. Was it rebellion, acceptance? Where were they going? To give birth, to give milk? Were they going to the altar, to the abattoir?

I was inside. And all the books were one single book, the primary school books, high school books, the book of dances, the book of fairies.

Arachnids, climbing down from the cupboard, were, at that moment, making the thread with which they'd reach the floor.

Mama was completely still; she wasn't doing any work; she had a brown freckle on her face, and some forget-me-nots in her hair.

* * *

I went outside; I stripped off; I began to spin; a beam of colours appeared; it folded round me; I ran; I seemed to be flying; I was flying along the ground; distant neighbours, close neighbours, known, unknown, came out to look at me, they were screaming: "Come back!" "Eh!" "You're crazy!" "Where are you going?" "To harvest the lilies?" "Are mushrooms sprouting backwards?" "Are you crazy?" "She was always crazy!"

Though I'd never done anything crazy. During my journey wings sprouted from me, at once completely pink and completely light-blue. Completely pink and, at once, completely light-blue. Stiff and turned like pieces of furniture. With them, in a few minutes, I'd reached the horizon.

And when I was about to disappear beyond it, my father caught me, held me tight; I was carried, again, to the kitchen, they gave me the dish of milk and potatoes. They said: Little one, don't run like that again.

At that moment a tiny butterfly came in and began spinning and spinning; it was pink and simultaneously, blue. At the same time, pink. At the same time, blue.

I was about to alert those nearby. But instead, I simply lowered my eyes.

* * *

As a little girl, I was a gypsy. I was called Turmalina. I sat down beside the path. And when the ladies went by, four or five of them, friends of my mother, always the same ones, all together, or just one, (or always the same one), I would say: Would you like me to tell your fortune?

In exchange, they would give me a warm, new-laid egg, or a bunch of green beans, things like that, which I paid no attention to, since I'd grown up with them.

But, when I was older, I found a spot on the roads, and when the gentlemen went by, I would say: Would you like me to tell you your fortune?

And they fled, at once slightly fascinated and frightened. (That's the woman only the wind has touched).

Still, now, my cousins return to the old farmhouse, and hear voices murmuring: A prophetess lived here.

* * *

When I was very little I asked mama: What's that?

And she answered: It's a broom.

And I said: What's a broom?

– Some bush tied to a stick, fitted with threads; and it's used to clean the house.

I replied with a laugh:

– Before I was born, I had a broom . . . silver-coloured. I remember it, perfectly. With it I went wherever I wanted to in a minute.

Mama went red as a beetroot; tiptoed about. And asked:

– You . . . what were you like . . . before . . . you were born?

I said: I was tall and very beautiful. The other girls didn't like me, they hated me; they pretended to be making jokes, laughing, but, I didn't care. I wore a lilac dress, a green shawl, pointy hat, and in a minute went wherever I wanted to.

Mama kept on and on like a dummy, out of her wits.

– You . . . what were you like . . . before . . . you were born?

I answered:

– I was called Turmalina. I had long long almond-coloured hair. And . . .

But that was all I told her about myself.

* * *

It's raining. It's night. As a result, our cousin Poupée will stay and sleep with us. It's raining. Someone says: No need to water the violets.

As always, for supper we'll eat rice with peas. As always.

I'm shaking. Because behind the cupboard there's a bat.

I tremble. Because this bat is mine.

Though it's not known who it will suck tonight.

For now, Poupée laughs. And I laugh.

* * *

It was an autumn out of all proportion. On the trunks, gigantic daisies of an exquisite orange colour burst open, (from the trunks!), and mushrooms, also gigantic, opened like umbrellas, and spoke to the passers-by who didn't show any surprise. On the contrary, they said to each other: "The mushroom told me that . . ." – "Listen to what those mushrooms think".

In the powerful insubstantial breeze, eagles carried out feats. They lifted a chicken into the sky and brought it down without doing it any harm. A new born "mulita" armadillo, only a few centimetres, grew in one minute to the size of a house; its brown carapace turned mother-of-pearl, became trails of thick pearls; its beauty was such you couldn't look at it. Luckily it dug down and escaped.

The apples took on a very intense vermillion red; they looked like round devils; they changed to a dazzling blue and to the colour of a star; they gave off sparks.

One of our cousins took the risk and ate one, and her skin became speckled with very faint grains of gold, that never went away. She lost her name and was called "Fairy".

So autumn passed. And the last thing that happened was, one calm midday, the house lifted; and we went on having lunch among the clouds. Next it deftly went down between the trees, and settled into its place. Some time later, our father stripped these events of all veracity. While our cousin "Fairy" energetically confirmed them.

* * *

I saw a very tall tree that was green and sombre-rose. The wind spun all the other trees from side to side; but it left this one standing there motionless. It seemed to have alcoves, bedrooms, sleeping people and dead people, vases with roses.

I was about to alert those in my vicinity; on the other hand, I went about this cautiously; I took my cape, my slippers. I thought the tree was going to flee; but no; it stayed still. I climbed up a few of its steps. A flock of hummingbirds flew away, but, as if they were scrawny, made of paper, though their colours were very bright.

In the tree, the people stayed motionless with a fake smile on their faces. I too found a spot and stretched out. Roses, honeysuckles, fell on my forehead and at my feet. The wind set the rest of the trees trembling. Of the house where I was born and grew up, I no longer remembered anything.

* * *

Instead of hair she had roses; little pink roses with short stems and green leaves. She had a bob of roses. And two centimetres above her head floated another pink rose with green leaves. This rose went with her always. Her face was oval, her eyes, almost unmoving. She wore a loose, pale-green coat, which was what girls on the farms usually wore. Mama, unexpectedly, invited her to have tea, saying she was the daughter of a distant relation; something that surprised me; I didn't know that. My friends laughed when they saw her. She sat down at the table, like the Virgin. She took what mama gave her: a cup with honey, tiny leaves of wallflower.

She left at sunset; maybe she had nothing to say to us.

She walked away surrounded by the timid smiles of my friends.

As if the roses were guiding her.

JORGE PALMA

PARAPHERNALIA

I haven't put on
my ears this morning
however
the world is stunning me,
its multitude of chairs
tied together,
its stock-market crashes,
that grinding of teeth
amid new shoes
and banknotes.

I think, with bullish insistence,
on what side of life
has life ended up?

The leopard skin
is trading on the market
at the price of a diamond.

Down the helter-skelter of fire
slide the passionate kisses
of lovers
falling into the spell of dark stars
with the cold days that wander
without a motherland

through tense cities
crammed with rubble.

No one whistles on the streets anymore.
And it seems embarrassing to long
for the calm blue sky
the yellow sound of wheat
the movement of water
in perfect circles
when a pebble
is thrown by a child
from the brightly-lit window of his room.

The pigeon returning
to the laid table
brings in its bloodied beak
a slap from the world.

How will I know from which direction
death will come.

THE BIRTH OF THE MOON

And here lies the sea
the sea where the stench of cities
comes to shine like stars.

V. Huidobro

The sky is black
and the shirts
hanging on a wire
are ruined in the discomfort
of funeral parlours.

In this unlikely morning
(half the sky
weeps buckets, in the other half
two suns sing like goldfinches)
I take a step
to recompose myself.

In my left pocket
a beaver weighs heavily
breathing, below my eyes
a clear morning
turns its back to the tar
gluing up the estuaries.

I put myself back together
gazing at the divided sea since my body
is in seven unequal parts.

The moon goes by nervously
smoking, down the corridors
of the ocean.

The asbestos cities
shine like wax candles
in the clenched hands of the dead.
And I'm hoping.

THE DROWNED

If there was fire, it would burn the earth;
If wind, it would raze it;
If water, it would drown it;
If God, he would sink it.

Cecco Anglioleri (1260 – 1313)

And with my eyes I listen to the dead.
Francisco Quevedo

There's a dead man in the depths
of the sky who can't get out
or drum the way he wants to
because it's raining outside
and everything is drowned.

That's why he strokes his forehead,
his cheeks, his three-day-old beard
and walks in circles
round his coffin, looking sideways
at the blue alpaca coat
without blinking
because outside it's raining and everything
below the sky is drowned.

And the drowned watch
the dark water drift towards
the unreachable depths of a red sunset

and they lean, they stretch on their side to listen,
they walk on tiptoes
because below the dogs are howling
in the place where mud is born.

And if there was wind
and it razed it;
and if there was fire
and it burnt everything?
someone asks
at the sky's request,
on behalf of the dead.

But I listen to the dead
singing into the small hours
and the drowned of the final
kingdom paddling about,
their souls in their arms, howling
from one side to the other of the sky.

And if there was wind
and it razed it;
if there was fire
and it burns everything?
asks the poet.

On behalf of the howling dogs
and the bones,
at the light's request,

and on behalf of
all the dead of this world
who can't get out
or play the drums the way they like
or the castanets
because outside wild rain is falling
and everything is drowned.

THE WORKING CLASS DON'T GO TO PARADISE

The working class don't go to paradise –
they travel crammed into the entrails
of a thunderbolt or worse: inside the wing-blow
of a lightning flash, slender-bodied,
bold-faced, or topless.

The working class knit the sky's wounds
in the workshops of time
as well as on looms, dreaming,
depending on who reads this and where, depending on
who hears this, who understands it,
what might be their personal flag
or the homeland's flag, the north
of each individual, their entire life.

Depending on who's looking at it, how it's seen.
Here or in China the working class
do not go to paradise: they travel in torment
in the entrails of a lightning bolt crammed
inside the entrails of a chicken
struck dumb in the wingless breeze
which with a soundless blow
evaporates in the air
as a flash of lightning evaporates
in the heavy air of a storm

and vanishes
amid the old looms
of the sky.

IMMORTALS

Those who at the request of darkness
go up to the platforms
and before the towers of heaven
justify their skimpy salary.

Those who, knowing in advance
that they will lose everything including their lives,
take charge of their discontent
and stand up,
walking down the streets
beating their chests,
covering billboards in the slogans of blood.

Those who despite fear
lack of faith
globalization
and uncertainty
go on believing in the heart's reasons
eternal love
and absolutes.

Those who blinded by
incomprehension's light
continue sowing daisies.

Those who were struck
by lightning and fire
and never cease
feeding doves.

Those who build plazas with hammocks
where people once rigged up bombs.

Those who shake away the dust
from abandoned tables
and lay out the tablecloth with 100 plates.

Those who wash the flags
(even though protocol says the opposite)

Those who shit on protocols.

Those who get married 17 times
so that love may be everlasting.

Those who hold out against the prod
the camp
the submarine
and returning to life
qualify as teachers
and build a school.

Those who
despite universal deafness
construct musical instruments.
Those who believe the sea
doubles as a handkerchief.

Those who believe it's possible
to paint stars on the distant sky.

Those who believe the sky
is not so distant
and sometimes, on extraordinary occasions,
can be touched by the hand.

Those who love too much
and instead of adopting
Vietnamese children
go out to the suburbs
to work with those who have no sky.

Those who build boats in the desert.

Those who paint birds
in jail.
Those who dream of flying
with the birds.
Those who dream.
Those whose heads
are filled with birds.

Those who keep birds
in their heads.

Those who consider wrinkles
on the skin as decorations.

Those who cry each time
an old man dies
because at that moment one more library
goes up in flames.

Those who forsake comfort
and a warm stove
and, in a full-on asthma attack,
walk off into the forest
to change everything.
To change everything.
To change it.

SALARIES

Is the salary of an ant
the same as that of a drug trafficker?

And that of a parish priest/ a nun/
a bishop/ a cardinal on fire?

Who pays? Who gives orders?

Is the salary of a hitman
the same as that of a doctor
a postman / a baker /
the same as an old
mournful gravedigger?

Who pays? Who gives orders?

What salary does God get
for administering the tasks
of the world?

Who pays? Who gives orders?

Who pays God?

CHILD AND LEOPARD

If with a mere
snap of the fingers
I could prevent you from suffering. . .
Or with my shoulder
brush aside your obligatory quota of pain;
whether you move this way or that
the iron clouds destined for each of us,
will drench us in either case.

Neither can I teach you
what fear is, since sooner or later
you'll understand it yourself,
though maybe you'll manage
to endure it in some
less dramatic way
than did your parents
grandparents, and distant ancestors
whom you will never meet.

Maybe then you will discover
that you've got saved up for you
a real fistful of wrinkles
and premature grey hairs
that come like a factory stamp.

For now I watch you drawing
with the assurance of a pure artist
driven only by the dazzling
of a world you've just begun to know.

Outside the leopard goes by,
silent and hard as a diamond.

Meanwhile, my daughter,
I look after your wings
and pray that you don't miss anything,
especially air and likewise
your joy which I defend
at whatever price
though it cost me my own light.

This is the time
we are summoned to live.

Outside the room
the leopard goes by
and the square where the hammocks swing
is empty.

It's cold
and I watch you drawing
on the misted glass of your window:
a house with its chimney,
a flower,

a yellow bird crossing
(so you say)
the sky of your room.

And I can't teach you
what fear is or stop you
from suffering, my dearest one, even if I drag
the sky and its clouds
somewhere else,
even if I take in
your share of destined rain
with this body wasted by love and years.

All the same
I'll try with a snap of the fingers
and see if I succeed.

FLORENCE

Cecilia, Florence is full
of beggars, not beggars with violets
like me,
but austere counts with fallen capes,
retired generals, hitmen
in mourning outside casinos
where crazed girls dream
in drunken stupor
of some white house shining
in the moon's gardens.

Cecilia,
the world is a table of wretched
tin, riddled with loneliness
and egotism,
the bleak deck of a ship
where a drunken man staggers
but doesn't fall,
mutters monosyllables,
hangs from the railings
when everything turns upside down
and he doesn't know if the sea is flying
or the exhausted stars have sunk
and it pains him to breathe
and he doesn't know if he's died
or just been born

because he can't wake up
and he's weeping.

Florence isn't Damascus
or Morocco or Andalusia,
it's a museum of pink stone
where I rot,
a monument to the loneliness
of art,
a mausoleum of yellow fever
convulsed by the insolent rain
of tourists.

And I'm exhausted from paddling against the flow.

And tonight in some dark way
demons surround me
as my blood shivers
and a sinister bird
crosses my forehead,
I'm nailed in the throat
by your joy
and the world is so large and wide
my love
that if you died
I couldn't close your eyes
with a howl
or beat like a madman
against the closed door of your coffin,

from the other side of
this table of cheap tin
where I write
to stop myself dying
and so that you
won't die.

THE LIGHTHOUSE AT THE END OF THE WORLD

Now we are at the ultimate end of the earth. . .
in an inaccessible wasteland.

Aeschylus

I've turned and seen it
anchored to the depths
of my eyes,
where night ends
and mists begin:

a blackened dog
beaten over and over
by the wild frenzy of petrol,

a dog whose hair is all bristles
barking with crazed abandonment.

And no one answers.

EVERYDAY LIFE

One would like to die
for each one of the dead
of this world
nevertheless it's never happened
that way

One runs to the nearest
chemist to salve
an everyday wound
or feels like savouring
his short holiday by the sea
while his nearest and dearest's heart
is shipwrecked
or on the fifth row
of the housing block
a small girl brings into the world
a thin root of light
or maybe rain
in quantities
never imagined before
not even
in the worst nightmares
of the flesh.

WIDE RIVER WITH AUTUMN FRAGRANCE

From red to green yellow dies.

APOLLINAIRE

You with the latest essential
glittering on your lapel,
do you even know what day it is?

In my pockets
the smell of damp earth
brings news from the world:
between red and green
yellow dies;
between my house and the shops
children die
in the desert.

The news speaks of war
and the sky moves forward.
The news talks of sandstorms
in the desert
and birds migrate
in my autumn sky.

While I light a cigarette
while the clothes

dry in the sun
children die
in the desert.

From red to green
yellow dies.

And the houses are abandoned
by their owners,
and widows leave flowers
on the middle of their beds
and walk away,
their skin covered
in widows' rags
in handkerchiefs of mourning
clothes of smoke
and they walk
along the sky's edge
and they walk by the shores
of the world.

On my patio with its pots
flowers fall from the sky
and birds fall
transfixed by the sounds of war,
and mothers wake up
under a changed sky
and in the marketplaces
fruit, fish,

the cries of people buying and selling,
don't bear the weight of any
sound of grief,
there are no widows
fleeing to the frontiers
and no earthquakes
and no one removes ground-up glass
from their shirt-sleeves
and priests don't sweep rubble
out of churches and cathedrals
and in my autumn sky
this morning I don't contemplate
the enormous journeys
of coffins and handkerchiefs
that in some place in the world
will fall apart; dust, sand,
burning desert,
where they say Paradise was,
the longed-for about-to-vanish Paradise
where a child still dreams
he has arms,
a family and legs,
the restless legs of a twelve-year-old child
who runs across immense sands,
leaps, looks for clouds,
defies the laws of physics, dreaming
in the lands of Ur
in the tremendous shadow
of a ruined Babylon.

From red to green
yellow dies.

Between your breast and mine
yellow dies.
Between your wings and my sleep
yellow dies.
Between your legs
and mine
autumn dies,
in four metres of sky
where four drops of rain
or dew
are falling,
three days from a blind
blast of gunfire,
in two minutes of glory
or disaster,
in one second of watching
dawn fall drop by drop
your mouth of light
your cry
to counterbalance perhaps
the scream soaring without pause
between two rivers
that carry death,
this howling that comes to us
across skies
storms dry heat,

a scream that crosses
the desert, your heart
your dwelling place
and like a steel fist
pounds against
the windows of my room,
here, in my small
autumn sky,
too far
from the freshly shaven men
who will never return home,
from women
chatting in a shop door
not knowing that tonight
they will sleep with death,
from those who have sung in the shower
for the last time, beautiful songs
gathered from twenty centuries,
those who never knew of us
and this river
or the name of the river
that names and crosses us
with its gentle identity.

Here in the South
where we grow old
watching the sunsets.

NARCISSUS AND THE RUBBISH DUMP

The world is one giant Narcissus
who is thinking of himself.

Joachin Gasquet

Like a prince in mourning
he walks the loneliness
along the world's shores
stepping over circles of fog
reliquaries
skeletons of seaweed
amulets
among candelabra
their shapes buried
and blue strips of cloth
that once were clothes
or doves
among sparks of marble
that were
staircases or sanctuaries
baptismal fonts
or sepulchres of angels
or suicides
who at some time
under the sky's clock
quietly urinated
in the deserted fountain
of a plaza.

Nevertheless
a sound penetrates
his forehead
a wild fury echoes
somewhere in the sky
and dies fallen
at his feet;
a wounded moon, open as a bird,
a living sore of three weeks
torn apart
between stones and snails
between scraps of doves
or clothing
among bottles
floating down
to the wild sea
still holding the sound
of rain or life;
seeds from ancient paradise
lidless eyes
that watch him go past
brooding and shivering
under a bleeding sun
plummeting.

AFTERWARDS

Later than so much
after everything
we will have to name
each thing
as if for the first time,
after lightning
and fire
after everything,
humbly,
silently,
at a leaden pace
and with a demiurge's patience,
among the corpses of stars
and the garbage.

ABOUT THE AUTHORS AND TRANSLATOR

OLGA OROZCO (1920-1999) was born in Toay, La Pampa, Argentina, spent her childhood in Bahía Blanca and at sixteen moved with her family to Buenos Aires. Her first collection of poems *Desde lejos* appeared in 1946 and was followed over the next five decades by nine further collections, as well as selected anthologies, two collections of short stories, essays and plays. Among other honours Olga Orozco was awarded the Juan Rulfo Prize for Latin American and Caribbean Literature in 1998.

MAROSA DI GIORGIO (1932-2004) was born in Salto, Uruguay. The child of first and second generation Italian immigrants, Di Giorgio grew up on a small farm on the city's outskirts. In 1953 her first book of poems appeared followed regularly by many others. From 1971 onwards her poetic work has been gathered into one continuously – expanding, thematically –interrelated book *Los papeles salvajes* – some 650 pages in its 2008 edition. Di Giorgio received a range of major awards for her poetry and presented her work at Festivals in Latin America, Spain and the United States.

JORGE PALMA (1961-) was born in Montevideo, Uruguay. He has worked in journalism and radio in the field of literary and cultural criticism. His first collection of poems *Entre el viento y la sombra* was published in 1989 and has been followed by four later collections. His poetry has been included in several anthologies and presented at numerous poetry festivals in Europe and Latin America. A collection of his short stories, *Paraísos artificiales*, was published in 1990.

PETER BOYLE is an Australian poet and translator of poetry from Spanish and French. As a poet his works include *Ghostspeaking* (2016), *Towns in the Great Desert* (2013) and *Apocrypha* (2009). In 2013 he was awarded the New South Wales Premier's Prize for Literary Translation. He is particularly noted for his translations of Cuban poet José Kozer and Venezuelan poet Eugenio Montejo.